Marketing Health Care into the Twenty-First Century
The Changing Dynamic

Marketing Health Care into the Twenty-First Century
The Changing Dynamic

Alan K. Vitberg

Routledge
Taylor & Francis Group
New York   London

First published by
The Haworth Press, Inc., 10 Alice Street, Binghamton, NY 13904-1580

This edition published 2013 by Routledge

Routledge
Taylor & Francis Group
711 Third Avenue
New York, NY 10017

Routledge
Taylor & Francis Group
2 Park Square, Milton Park
Abingdon, Oxon OX14 4RN

Routledge is an imprint of the Taylor & Francis Group, an informa business

Library of Congress Cataloging-in-Publication Data

Vitberg, Alan K.
    Marketing health care into the twenty-first century : the changing dynamic / Alan K. Vitberg.
        p.   cm.
    Includes bibliographical references and index.
    ISBN 1-56024-979-X (alk. paper)
    1. Medical care United States Marketing. 2. Managed care plans (Medical care)–United
States. I. Title.
RA410.56.V58 1996
362.1′068′8 dc20   95-44795
                                                                                              CIP

To my adorable wife Janice and my beautiful children, Sarah and Shannon:

Thanks for giving me the time,
Thanks for giving me the quiet,
Thanks for giving me the support,
Thanks for putting up with the grumpiness.

Il est fini!

ABOUT THE AUTHOR

Alan K. Vitberg, MBA, is President of The Crestwood Group (Rochester, New York), a management consulting firm specializing in strategic, marketing, and business assessment and planning services to health care providers and payers. He has provided market research, detailed competitive analysis, preparation of strategic, tactical, and business/operational plans for the development and launch of health maintenance organizations, independent practice associations, physician/hospital organizations, physician organizations, and management service organizations, among other services.

CONTENTS

List of Figures

List of Tables

Acknowledgments

Many people and organizations contributed to making *Marketing Health Care into the Twenty-First Century* a reality.

First and foremost, I would like to thank my wife Janice Vitberg, who not only put up with my seven-days-a-week, fourteen-hours-a-day routine during the writing of this book, but who also served as Research Assistant, Executive Assistant, Secretary, Proofreader, and Gofer. Without her contributions, this book would not have been possible, and her patience, understanding, and encouragement were invaluable. From countless hours on the phone setting up interviews to scrambling to the library to acquire reference materials to making sure that I stopped every once in a while to eat, Janice was a major contributor.

Next, I would like to thank my partner and friend Leon Gossin, who gracefully took on more burdens of The Crestwood Group as I devoted time to *Marketing Health Care*. Leon's encouragement and support were key to the attitude I brought to writing this book; his willingness to serve as a sounding board for ideas and concepts was invaluable, and at long last I don't have to answer the question, "You're on what page????" Thanks, Leon; now we again devote 100 percent of our time and attention to helping our clients "hit 'em where they ain't."

I would also like to thank the people who took time from their busy schedules to spend a few moments talking about changes in the health care industry. They include: John Urban, CEO of Preferred Care; Mike Honig, President of American Health Management and Consulting Corporation; Nancy Connelie of HealthSource Maine; Terry Friedlander of FHP; Jim Epple of Allina Health System; and Rick Wade of the American Hospital Association. Also, my thanks to a number of organizations who contributed materials: the Medical Group Management Association; Group Health Association of America; Health Insurance Institute of America; and Interstudy Publications.

Of particular note, Roger Gates, President of DSS Research in Arlington, Texas, provided a number of critical insights, particularly in regard to the state of branding in the health care industry and product development opportunities using conjoint analysis. Roger is one of the finest market research authorities in health care today, and an incredible guide to the best Mexican restaurants in the Dallas/Fort Worth area.

Last, but not least, I would like to acknowledge all of the payers, physicians, and hospitals who are living within the changing dynamic. Together, you are responsible for the health care of 240 million Americans. Your job is tough, and is being made even tougher by market and cost pressures for a quality product at a reasonable cost. It is my hope that this book will, in some small measure, help you turn chaos into opportunity.

Introduction:
Revolution or Evolution?

At the world headquarters of my company, The Crestwood Group, we've built a small shrine to Bill and Hillary Clinton. Every day, before work, we gather around this shrine and pay silent thanks—not because of the consulting work generated prior to the demise of the Health Security Act (although it sure did pay the mortgage and orthodontist bills), but because they lit a fuse, which fizzled legislatively, that has led to an explosive market-based revolution in the health care industry. We're now busier and more involved in strategic and market planning for physicians, hospitals, and payers than we've ever been in the history of our company. So, in the way of introduction, I (and I assume many of my marketing peers) would like to formally thank and acknowledge the progenitors of our collective heavy workload, the Clinton Administration.

Thank you. You've given us the opportunity to be gainfully employed far into the foreseeable future.

The national focus on health care reform highlighted publicly what many of us knew privately—that health care is too expensive; its practitioners suffer a lack of fiscal accountability; it's a nightmare from administrative and information technology perspectives; too many people lack even the most basic insurance coverages; and there is a cornucopia of villains contributing to problems in the industry from malpractice litigators to high tech companies to experience-based insurance rating practices. As a matter of fact, the list of villains probably encompasses just about anybody and everybody associated with health care, including patients.

In moving toward a solution, a funny thing happened. While a legislative answer to health care problems was soundly thrashed at the national level, the market spoke. It said, "We're not gonna take it anymore. . . . You're too expensive and we can't afford it! Cut your costs or suffer the wrath of our combined purchasing clout."*

It appears that the industry is responding. According to a survey done by Foster Higgins[1], health care costs for employers decreased 1.1 percent in 1994 when compared with 1993, attributable largely to an increase of employee enrollment in managed care plans.

Marketers should and must play key, critical roles in the industry's continuing response to market-driven pressures. A key conclusion of this book is that the health care marketer of the future must possess a combination of skills and attitudes–visionary; entrepreneur; sales manager; strategic planner; medical director; behavioral psychologist; lawyer; actuary; accountant and more–all in addition to the "normal" marketing roles, responsibilities, and demeanor that marketers bring to the office every day.

THE CHANGING DYNAMIC'S SUBJECT

The intention of this book is to describe the chaotic, changing landscape of health care in America and its implications for health care marketing and marketers; and in the process, provide guidance on how to turn this chaos into opportunity.

In terms of a product, "health care" is truly amorphous–it can be anything from an over-the-counter cold remedy to an insurance product. It can be a service, like pain management or home health care. It can be positioned and promoted from tangible perspectives such as price or outcomes to intangible perspectives seeking to establish affinity with the goals, motivations, or values of prospects.

The product this book addresses is the *health care plan or system*–a product with both medical delivery and insurance components (administration, finance, sales) whose mission is to address both the financial security and the wellness, nonacute, acute, and catastrophic health care needs of its customers. This product has

---

* In Rochester, New York, for example, even though the community's health care cost containment activities have been nationally acclaimed, the Industrial Management Council (a group driven by large employers in the market) has taken a position that ". . . by 1998, (health care insurance) premium increases *will not exceed* the Consumer Price Index."

traditionally been rooted in insurance, with medical delivery participants seen as vendors rather than partners.

*In the changing dynamic, everybody–physician, hospital, and
payer–is a marketer, with responsibilities for positioning, packaging, pricing, and promoting the health care system.*

This book is not just for marketers in the health insurance industry.
As markets and health care plan structure evolve, physicians and
hospitals *must* incorporate a marketing mentality in their strategic
thinking based upon a simple premise: you are a product; a product
that must be packaged, priced, positioned, and promoted to managed
care organizations in order to ensure your survival. The marketing
process faced by providers is complex, driven by the need to consolidate into ever increasingly large medical delivery organizations.

Much of the consolidation activity is being driven by financial
concerns. What is suggested herein is that marketing concerns–for
example, the need to differentiate, the need to create and sustain
competitive advantage, the need to capture and retain market share,
the need to create a branded identity, and so on–occupy a position in
the strategic thinking of providers equal in importance to financial
concerns.

Marketing Health Care into the Twenty-First Century, therefore,
should be of appeal to a wide audience in the health care industry.
For physicians, this book delivers insights on how external pressures are changing their profession, clout they possess, and opportunities for leveraging that clout through strategic and operational
marketing activities. Physicians represent the greatest degree of
fragmentation in the industry both in terms of conflicting interests
(primary care versus specialist; solo versus group; self-employed
versus employed, and so on) and lack of strong, centralized planning and financial management organizations. This book not only
shows why, from a marketing perspective, physicians should organize, but also, how that organization can occur.

For hospitals, this book addresses their evolving role in the health
care system, the current pressures and threats they face, and market-
ing-based strategies and activities that can help negate those threats.
Hospitals appear to be at the most risk in the changing environment
of health care. At worst, the hospital's survival, and at best, its
prosperity, will be a function of strategic and tactical marketing

activities coordinated through and from CEO to COO (Chief Operating Officer) to CFO (Chief Financial Officer) to Medical Departments. The window of opportunity for hospitals to retain the status quo is swiftly eroding in many markets. This book delivers insights, from a marketing perspective, on how to keep the window open.

For payers, *Marketing Health Care* discusses different types of marketing activities dependent upon managed care penetration, with particular attention paid to how financial and risk considerations, in conjunction with brand and product development, can lead to sustainable competitive advantage. More than ever before, CEOs, senior marketing managers, product managers, Medical Directors, physician relation managers, and customer service personnel must read and respond to changing market dynamics in order to meet market demand.

Finally, this book will give policymakers, investors, and just about anybody else interested in the health care industry an opportunity to understand industry dynamics from a marketer's perspective. As may be inferred from the above, the potential for conflict between and among the key participants in the industry is great, and while this book does not give preferential treatment or consideration to any one type of participant, it does suggest that there will be winners and losers within each local health care market. No one participant has achieved a clear sustainable advantage, but by understanding and responding to market dynamics, it is possible to achieve and maintain a dominant position in the market in terms of share, control, and voice.

KEY PREMISES

There are seven key premises underlying *Marketing Health Care:*

1. The changing dynamic is a war zone characterized by battles between and among payers, physicians, and hospitals for enrollees, patients, and health care dollars.

If there is one key theme expressed throughout this book, it is that the health care industry is in a war that will only increase in fervor and intensity as organizations fight for survival and the capture of hundreds of billions of dollars. While I might be accused of not being "PC" (Professionally Correct), one need only to look at what is happening in local markets across the country to see the truth in this characterization, from closure of hospitals to primary care physicians selling their practices to bitter fights between payers for managed care enrollment.

Although it may sound harsh and extreme, those payers and providers who understand that they're fighting a war and act accordingly stand the best chance of short-term survival and long-term prosperity. Those that do not act accordingly, burying their heads in the sand awaiting the storm of war to blow over, will find themselves prisoners of their inactivity. Others will become causalities on the altar of altruism, bemoaning the fact that "health care is supposed to be driven by concern for people, not finances."

In this book, the battlefields of the changing dynamic will be described, and strategies and tactical insights—for both payer and provider—will be delivered. For the health care marketer, not only will it become increasingly critical to obtain the intelligence necessary for a successful "campaign," but also, to have weapons, from branding tactics to product mix and more, at the ready.

As in any war, some battles will be won, others lost, and in the process there will be casualties, survivors, and victors. Payers will battle for market share, hospitals will battle for survival, and physicians will battle for autonomy and lifestyle maintenance. There will be fighting between payers and hospitals, between payers and physicians, between hospitals and physicians, between hospitals, and between physicians in the changing dynamic.

2. Managed care is the single largest force on the health care battlefield today and for the foreseeable future.

The growth of managed care has been phenomenal over the past twenty years, and it is expected that managed care enrollment will continue to rise dramatically over the foreseeable future. Managed care is affecting the way customers perceive and purchase health insurance. It has created sophisticated buyers demanding quality outcome at reasonable prices. It is seen as a panacea for high cost government programs (Medicare and Medicaid). It has spawned the need for sophisticated information systems. Perhaps most important, it has driven the need for new types of relationships between payers and providers.

Historically, an arm's length relationship has characterized most payer/provider relationships and, ultimately, it has been the payer who has been accountable for pricing, packaging, and promoting a product to customers. Tomorrow, because managed care pressures will favor those entities that can deliver a comprehensive, high-quality, low-cost product, relationships among and between players in the health care industry will undergo a radical metamorphosis. This metamorphosis will affect and is affecting structural, operational, clinical, financial, and marketing relationships between payers and providers. In fact, as a consequence of managed care, payers and providers have increasingly become dependent upon one another with the ultimate responsibility of structuring and delivering a product with broad appeal to consumers.

As this metamorphosis occurs, the health care marketer's roles and responsibilities within the organization will likewise change.

Chapter 1, The Changing Dynamic, describes and discusses characteristics and key trends driving the health care industry over the last thirty years, with particular attention paid to managed care and its implications for the health care marketer.

3. Three different types of health care battlefields, or markets, can be defined on the basis of managed care penetration and the effect of that penetration upon intra- and inter-provider relationships, and provider/payer relationships.

Analysts such as Kaiser and Risk[2] maintain that health care is a local business and that the market for health care services is not national in nature. As managed care penetration increases within a local market, market dynamics change, and as dynamics change, so too do the strategic marketing issues, needs, objectives, and target markets of the health care marketer. Local markets have gone through evolutionary stages and will continue to do so—a process described in this book and expressed in terms of "battlefields."

To set the stage, these battlefields may be characterized as follows:

- A *First Generation Battlefield* is an *emerging market* characterized by low to below average managed care penetration; the dominance of cost-plus and fee-for-service reimbursement mechanisms; and arm's length relationships between payers and providers, each attempting to pursue and protect their self-interests in terms of market share, income, and profits. First Generation markets pit indemnity coverage against prepaid health care, where managed care marketers seek to motivate customers to accept restricted access to the medical delivery system for lower premium and out-of-pocket costs.
- A *Second Generation Battlefield* is a *consolidating market* characterized by above average managed care penetration; consolidations of providers into networks, alliances, partnerships, etc.; and new financial relationships with payers in terms of various risk-sharing mechanisms–all as a consequence of growing cost containment pressures driven by managed care. The Second Generation is a battlefield at the local level, where new organizations–particularly on the provider side–are being created with increasing intensity and fervor as physicians, physician organizations, hospital organizations, and physician/hospital organizations each attempt to secure a sustainable competitive advantage in the face of increasing cost pressures generated by managed care penetration.
- A *Third Generation Battlefield* is a *mature market* characterized by high managed care penetration, the creation of large health care systems where medical delivery and insurance functions are combined within one organization, and a reduction in numbers of competitors as smaller players are squeezed out of their market. In the Third Generation Market, large, self-contained health care systems battle against one another on the basis of brand differentiation and the ability to create and position differentiated products based upon the composition of their integrated medical delivery network.

A key feature of a Third Generation Battlefield is that from a utilization perspective, excess capacity and overutilization have, for the most part, been squeezed out of the market. Another feature centers around the size of competitors in the market, particularly from the perspective that size creates economies of scale (in terms of purchasing and overhead unit costs, which in turn, can impact product pricing) and the resources to quickly duplicate competitive product innovations. This basically means that for health care systems competing in this market, competition around costs and benefits may not be a viable marketing strategy. Yet, marketers on the Third Generation Battlefield will still need to drive preference and execute strategies designed to steal share from competitors.

It is not suggested that every local market will evolve or follow a linear path to the Third Generation. Some markets may continue to operate within a First or Second Generation environment for the foreseeable future, others may move quickly to maturity, and still others may find that there is no clear demarcation line between generations. It is very conceivable that some markets of the future will have elements of all three generations.

Chapter 2, Health Care Battlefields, describes characteristics and differences between the three generations of health care battlefields, or markets, including but not limited to managed care penetration, market structures and dynamics, and marketing needs, issues, and objectives characteristic of each type of market generation. This chapter will also deliver insights on how to recognize market structure and consequent strategic and tactical marketing activities.

4. On the battlefield, three different types of health care plan structures or systems exist.

Within any given market, one or more types of health care plan structures or systems can be identified:

- The *Autonomous Health Care Plan/Structure* can either be indemnity or managed care based but is mainly characterized by a contractually based, arms length relationship between the payer and providers. In this system, marketing functions are generally resident within the payer's organization, and the plan's product is strictly an insured product.
- The *Synergistic Health Care System* is managed care based, is still characterized by contractually based relationships between payers and providers, and insurance based products.

There are two key differences between this system and the Autonomous System: payers are now contracting with consolidating provider organizations who accept risk; and a concrete marketing function exists within the provider's domain pursuant to developing the system–those marketing functions and activities necessary for creating the consolidated medical delivery system or network and the subsequent "sale" of that network to multiple managed care organizations. However, the actual marketing of the system to customers is still resident within the payer's organization and the system marketer will have a very powerful tool at his disposal–the ability to create and position differentiated products based upon the composition of the integrated medical delivery network, opening opportunities for niche or segmented products.

Effectively, synergy is created by the cooperative actions of payers and providers in this system, such that the total effect of cooperation is greater than the sum of the effects independently. In fact, another characteristic of this system is decentralized accountability, in the sense that every single participating organization and employee of the system will ultimately be responsible for its success. Figure 1 presents a model of a Synergistic Health Care System.

- The *Homogenous Health Care System* is also managed care based and can be found within consolidating and mature markets. In this system, however, insurance and medical delivery functions are combined under one seamless umbrella or organizational entity, where medical delivery participants provide services exclusively to the system and where marketing functions are resident at the system level. In fact, it might be argued that staff model Health Maintenance Organizations (and to a lesser degree, group model HMOs) are characteristic of this system. However, the most likely route to a Homogenous System will be the merger of a large medical delivery system with a payer in the market.

  Now, the marketing function is resident at the health care system level, where marketers have pricing, packaging, and promotional responsibilities for the system, not just a health insurance plan. Of critical importance, the uniformity of this type of system creates unique opportunities for competitive differentiation, particularly in terms of the ability to brand the organization. Another distinct feature of the Homogenous System should be its ability to react swiftly to changing market dynamics as the organization should be able to act with one voice and through one purpose, rather than having to go through the motions of establishing new contractually based relationships to meet market needs. Speed, or the ability to act swiftly upon a need voiced by the market, is a critical tool in industries ruled by chaos.

We are witnessing an era where bigger is perceived as better, and where size translates into advantage in terms of being able to create and pass on cost savings as a function of economies of scale. Chapter 3, Health Care Plan Structures and Systems, describes characteristics and differences between these different health care plans, with particular attention paid to the relationship between market status and use of health care plan structure to create competitive advantage.

5. Victors in the changing dynamic will be those physicians, hospitals, doctors, and health care systems that can seize and maintain competitive advantage.

The fourth premise of this book is that seizing and maintaining competitive advantage is the key for thriving and prospering in the changing dynamic. Competitive advantage is a spirit, a behavior, a desire to win and to be the very best at what you do. It is an integral part of the essence and character of an organization, reflected in the quality of its services and products, in a belief in its services and products, and in the aggressiveness and willingness of employees to promote and sell the organization internally and externally.

Competitive advantage involves a willingness to aggressively fight for market share and position, for continually increasing sales, and for establishing irrevocable and unbreakable linkages between the organization and its customers. It requires a willingness to capitalize upon strengths of the organization and weaknesses of competitors. It means seizing opportunities or making opportunities to grow a category or drive preference. And, it involves an ability to recognize and respond to threats before they become a damaging

FIGURE 1. The Synergistic Health Care System

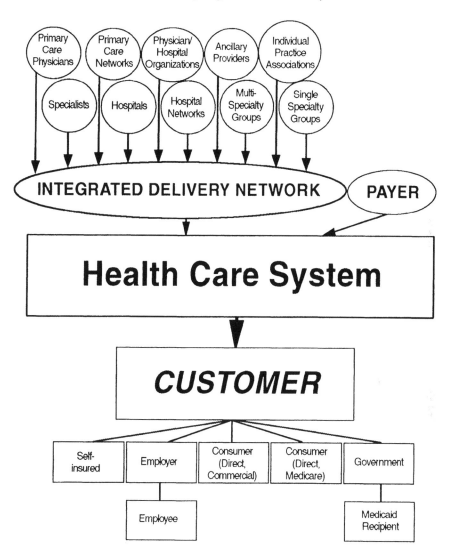

force. The desire for competitive advantage lies at the very core of the organization.

Chapter 4, Winning the War–Critical Factors for Success in the Changing Dynamic, explores the concept and components of competitive advantage.

6. Competitive advantage is a function of the presence and interrelationship of competitive innovation and market excitation.

The ability to create, secure, and sustain competitive advantage involves the interaction, integration, and blending of two groups or sets of activities. The internal set, *Competitive Innovation*, addresses the research, planning, branding, and positioning needs of the health care system for achieving competitive advantage. Competitive innovation is a process requiring the health care marketer's commitment and willingness to "break out of the box" of conventional thinking and norms. Chapter 5, Preparing for Battle–The Art and Process of Competitive Innovation, describes the elements of hearing, listening, and responding to the voice of the market.

The external set of activities, *Market Excitation*, represents those activities that are *directly* involved in creating awareness and driving preference. From customer service to marketing communications, Market Excitation activities represent the "face" of the organization to its prospects and customers, and create the environment and conditions for winning competitive advantage. Chapter 6, Fighting the Battle–The Art and Process of Market Excitation, discusses these activities in detail.

Competitive innovation and market excitation are integrally and fundamentally interconnected, and only when working in concert with one another can competitive advantage be produced. Figure 2 shows this interrelationship.

7. As markets evolve, as battles intensify and as new health care system structures are created, the roles and responsibilities of the health care marketer must also change and evolve.

Traditionally, marketers in the health care industry have held responsibilities for product development and launch. From the

FIGURE 2. Creating Competitive Advantage

Market Excitation

Marketing Communications

Hearing the Voice of the Market
Listening to the Voice of the Market
Responding to the Voice of the Market

Competitive Innovation

Market Intelligence
Competitive Intelligence
Positioning
Brand Identity
Planning

Product Mix

Customer Service

Expanded Distribution

Aggressive Sales Staff

payer's perspective, this translates into creating insured products around cost, benefit, and access variables. From the hospital's perspective, marketing has typically centered around promotion of services such as birthing centers or single specialty services such as occupational rehabilitation. From the physician's perspective, marketing has traditionally been ignored.

Taking the position that in the changing dynamic everybody is a marketer, and given a focus upon the health care system as the product, the roles and responsibilities of marketers must change, particularly as managed care pressures create new market dynamics and organizational structures. As markets evolve, the marketing function must be dedicated to strategic marketing analysis which will lead to creating relationships first, and based upon those relationships, creating products second. And, once relationships have been established, and excess capacity and utilization squeezed out of the market, influencing prospects to purchase may become a function of differentiation around access, composition of the medical delivery system, and brand identity.

Chapter 7, Conclusion, discusses the tools, responsibilities, and roles of the health care marketer of the future.

REFERENCE NOTES

1. Foster Higgins, *National Survey of Employer-Sponsored Health Plans 1994.*

2. R.R. Risk, "Multihospital Systems: The Turning Point" in *Topics in Health Care Financing*, Vol. 18, No. 3 (1992), pp. 46-53; and L.R. Kaiser, "The Future of Multihospital Systems" in *Topics in Health Care Financing,* Vol. 18, No. 4 (1992), pp. 32-45.

CHAPTER 1:
THE CHANGING DYNAMIC

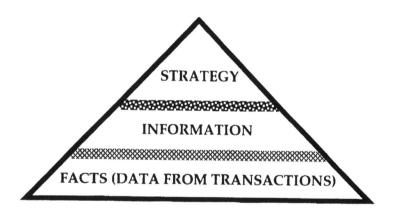

Where is the WISDOM we have lost in knowledge? *
Where is the KNOWLEDGE we have lost in intelligence?*
Where is the INTELLIGENCE we have lost in information?
Where is the INFORMATION we have lost in data?
Where are the DATA we have lost in ignorance?

Source: Vincent P. Barabba and Gerald Zaltman, *Hearing the Voice of the Market.*
Boston: Harvard Business School Press, 1991, pp. 41 and 46. Reprinted by
permission.
*T.S. Eliot, "The Rock."

Wars are often won or lost based upon intelligence gathered from the field. Commanders must be aware of both the big picture as well as specific battlefield conditions in order to develop successful strategies and tactics. They must have historical perspective as well as an uncanny ability to chart the future by understanding, recognizing, and responding to today's environment while spotting tomorrow's trends.

The health care marketer of today and tomorrow must serve a critical role of information gatherer and interpreter. Health care battles will be fought on the fields of managed care, integration, consolidations and mergers, and government programs, among others.

Consequently, more than ever before, providers and payers must listen to and correctly interpret the voice of the market. They must be fully attuned to the signals that come from customers and competitors in order to make the right decisions at the right time. Organizations that lose touch with the market, that either ignore or misinterpret its signals, will fail in today's and tomorrow's health care industry.

Barabba and Zaltman[1] maintain that competitive advantage lies in a process of hearing, listening, and responding to the voice of the market. In the health care industry, this voice tells us that change is occurring on an evolutionary scale on many fronts, from provider reimbursement methods to information needs and uses. Within this changing environment, the payer, medical delivery, and health care system marketer ultimately holds responsibility for making sure that customers understand the basic concept behind a product or service; showing customers the relevance of the product or service to their needs; and removing or significantly reducing barriers to transactions or exchanges so that customers can engage in a transaction with minimum effort.[2]

Like any evolution, industries evolve because forces are in motion, creating incentives or pressures to change.[3] Understanding these forces and their implications (i.e., "the voice of the market"), and creating strategically based, customer responsive products and services must lie within the domain of today's payer, medical delivery, and health care system marketers.

The beginning of the industry's evolutionary path can be traced to an era where fee-for-service for physicians and cost-plus-reimbursement for hospitals encouraged spending without recourse to efficiency. Free choice of provider and differential subsidies favoring inpatient hospital care began to contribute significantly to rising medical costs.[4] Faced with unlimited demand and the prospect of unlimited payment for the likely sickest of our population, commercialization of health care began in earnest.[5]

Motivated by a cost-based payment system and a price insensitive environment that encouraged and rewarded system growth,[6] the industry witnessed the rapid expansion of horizontally integrated multiple hospital systems. According to Fottler and Malvey, the pursuit of horizontal integration can be:

> . . . Attributed in part to hospitals' attempts to deal with an increasingly complex and often hostile environment that created intense financial pressures and risks that threatened institutional survival. System affiliation offered hospitals opportunities to reduce or diversify certain facility-specific risks. Hospitals could gain management expertise, access to capital, and improve their overall financial status through afflictions with well-managed, financially sound institutions.[7]

Horizontally integrated systems were expected to offer hospitals advantages ranging from economies of scale to increased political power, but ". . . the only advantage that system hospitals have demonstrated is an increase in labor productivity through more efficient use of personnel. . . . Because cost-based reimbursement offered few incentives to systems to operate efficiently, there were no rewards for reducing costs."[8] In fact, S.M. Shortell maintains that hospital systems have failed to fully integrate and have been unable to perform as systems rather than as collections of facilities, and that in order for a system to be fully and functionally integrated, both administrative and clinical services must be vertically integrated within the system.[9]

Stimulated by government and employer reactions to rising health care costs, and given momentum by Federal grants, managed care began to truly develop in the early 1970s. This process was a reaction to a flawed payment system that rewarded health professionals for utilization To this day, the echoes of this reaction reverberate in the hallways of providers and payers across the nation as providers and payers seek to position themselves to capitalize upon a growing demand for cost control.

Insurers began to manage their payments for health services, and found that in indemnity markets, the combination of minor changes in benefit structures and discounts from providers could produce astounding profits. The HMO Act of 1973, for example, was based on evidence that medical costs could be reduced with incentives to prevent and reduce hospitalizations.[10] Wolford, Brown, and McCool maintain that the emergence of HMOs:

> . . . Came at a time when health insurance companies were moving away from community-rated insurance to corporate or group rated insurance. The sense of community sharing of health care risk was being lost as corporations and other groups chose to reduce their health care costs by extracting themselves from the community pool. The focused marketing of HMOs toward young, healthy groups exacerbated the flight from the concept of community health. The results are massive cost shifting among buyers of health services and massive displacement of potential buyers of health insurance who are either deemed an unhealthy risk or insufficient in group size to be afforded affordable health care rates.[11]

Control over medical costs during the 1980s through the early 1990s focused upon component level cost control. According to John Eichert, President of Hastings Healthcare Group, under component level control, utilization management techniques are used to reduce the demand for individual products or services or to optimize utilization of appropriate resources. However, component management, maintains Hastings:

1. Emphasizes the treatment of disease rather than prevention which would avoid costly complications;
2. Wastes time, money, and human resources as a consequence of lack of coordination and continuity of treatment;
3. Shows a bias against expensive treatments that cost more in the short-term but save money in the long term;
4. Produces few provider incentives to treat the entire disease; and
5. Encourages an overall increase in utilization of services as a result of revenue based reimbursement.[12]

Concurrently, hospitals began to offer volume discounts under the assumption that economies of scale, afforded by size, would protect their market share. By the mid-1980s, however, declining demand, excess capacity, increased managerial control by managed care organizations, and continuing cost containment pressures magnified critical flaws in horizontal integration. This led to the development of national-scale *vertically* integrated systems, attempting to combining medical services and insurance under one umbrella.[13]

Thus, the structure of the health care industry has changed in fundamental ways, and as Michael Porter maintains, industry evolution takes on critical importance for formulation of strategy:

> Understanding the process of industry evolution and being able to predict change are important because the cost of reacting strategically usually increases as the need for change becomes obvious and the benefit from the best strategy is highest for the first firm to select it.[14]

Into the twenty-first century, participants on the battlefields of the health care industry will face the need to deal with a number of key trends that will determine whether they decline, survive, or thrive. These include:

- The growth of managed care
- The frenzy of provider integration activities
- Provider and payer consolidations and mergers
- The explosion of information and information technology
- Government initiatives to increase managed Medicare and Medicaid.

Each of these are explored in this chapter.

THE CONTINUED GROWTH OF MANAGED CARE

The growth of managed care has sparked evolution in clinical, financial, administrative, and strategic relationships between and among payers, physicians, and hospitals that must be incorporated into the strategic, tactical, and operational battle plans and activities of the payer, medical delivery, and health care system marketer of today. In particular, the evolution of managed care has fostered movements toward vertical integration and consolidations, mergers, and acquisitions. It has changed and expanded the scope of information needs and technologies. And, as a consequence of a perceived ability to cut costs, is driving Federal and state government to expand market opportunities through managed Medicare and Medicaid initiatives.

At the beginning of 1994, according to the Group Health Association of America, HMO enrollment was about 45 million, a 650 percent increase from the 6 million HMO enrollees of 1976.[15] During this same period, the number of HMOs increased from 175 to 556, peaking in 1988 where some 650 HMOs were serving some 32.7 million enrollees.[16] Regardless of model, the average annual growth rate for all HMOs is 10 percent.[17]

According to the *Foster Higgins National Survey of Employer Sponsored Health Plans/1994*, 37 percent of employees are in a traditional indemnity plan, and 63 percent are in plans with varying degrees of managed care (Foster Higgins: Princeton, NJ). Preferred Provider Organizations (PPOs), for example, enroll some 25 percent of employees, Point-of-Service Plans (POS) enroll 15 percent of all employees, and HMOs serve 23 percent of all employees. In comparison, data from a survey of members of the Health Insurance Association of America indicate that in 1990, 38 percent of employees were enrolled in managed care plans.[18] In 1987, this figure was 27 percent.[19]

From a commercial insurance perspective, market rather than legislative pressures are driving the growth of managed care. Employers are not waiting quietly for health care reform legislation, but are taking aggressive action to rein in health care costs, including introducing managed care alternatives, monitoring utilization, and demanding outcomes and utilization data.[20] Employers are trying to balance employee satisfaction with savings, want, convenience, and user-friendly systems for their workers, and access to rapid response to employee-patient needs.[21]

Recent studies show that on average, effective HMOs may reduce costs by 9 percent;[22] other researchers have reported larger savings of 15 to 25 percent relative to traditional fee for service.[23] GTE, for example, saw health care costs rise between 15 and 18 percent per year during the 1980s even with a self-funded indemnity plan served by one national insurer. After study, they concluded that health care works best as a local matter and that locally based staff model HMOs could best serve their employees health care needs.

To effect their decisions, GTE put HMOs through a rigorous information and assessment process; created a managed care group to serve as internal consultants across GTE business units; and created an integrated health care information system. According to George H. Crowling, a GTE Manager of Managed Care, "Our short term goal was to move people into HMOs and when we came in, in late 1991-early 1992, we had 32 percent of our active employees in HMOs. We now have 52 percent two years later. I am confident it will be 2 to 3 points higher in 1995."[24]

In 1990 Xerox Corp., with 11,000 out of its 55,000 employee workforce in some 200 HMOs, began its HealthLink program, implementing an ambitious strategy to move its employees from a self-funded indemnity plan into HMOs. By 1995, more than 70 percent of Xerox employees are enrolled in one of six different "HMO Networks" with true savings of about $1,000 annually.[25]

However, managed care growth is not being driven by employer cost concerns alone. Citing research accomplished by the Sachs Group Inc. and Scarborough Research Corp. that almost 70 percent of HMO members had a choice of plans (compared to 42 percent of fee for service and 41 percent of PPO members), Ann Mond Johnson, a Sachs Vice President, claims that "clearly, the growth in managed care in general and HMOs specifically is being driven by the consumer."[26] In effect, people are in HMOs because they want to be.

Yet, managed care penetration varies widely from state to state and market to market. Consider, for example, that ten states have managed care penetration rates of less than 5 percent. Conversely, fourteen states have penetration rates exceeding 20 percent. Figure 1.1 shows distribution of states by managed care penetration rate.

The *Sachs/Scarborough HealthPlus* study found that HMO members are more satisfied with their health plans than members of fee for service plans and PPOs, regardless of their health status. Fully 82 percent of HMO members are more satisfied with their plans, compared to 72 percent of people in FFS plans, and 71 percent of people in PPOs.[27]

FIGURE 1.1. Managed Care Penetration Rates by State

20%   25%   30%   35%   40%

Florida (20.1)
Ohio (20.4)
  Hawaii (21.5)
  Missouri (21.5)
      Connecticut (23.9)
          Wisconsin (25.7)
          Delaware (25.9)
        Utah (26.8)
            Rhode Island (27.6)
          Arizona (27.9)
        New York (28.3)
            Colorado (30.8)
                Minnesota (34.2)
                  California (36.9)
                  Maryland (37.3)
                      Oregon (39.6)
                          Massachusetts (40.2)

Managed care has had and will continue to have a dramatic impact on providers as well. For example, a recent report from the Sachs Group (*The National Bellweather Report*) finds that as a result of managed care:

- Inpatient hospital discharges will decrease. Discharges for 1993 were estimated at 32,996,380. Under a 100 percent managed care scenario in 1998, discharges will only be 26,044,660, a 21 percent decline.
- Managed care will dramatically reduce length of stay. In 1993, average length of stay was estimated at 6.04 days. In 1998, under 100 percent managed care, that figure is reduced to 3.55 days–a 41 percent decrease.
- As a result, there will be too many hospital beds. The supply of hospital beds in the United States is estimated at 1,117,850. Demand in 1993 was only 608,900. Under a 100 percent managed care scenario in 1998, the demand for beds is reduced to 504,760. Therefore, in 1998, we will only need 43 percent of the beds currently in existence.

These statistics do not paint a particularly bright picture for hospitals under managed care. As will be discussed in later parts of this and other chapters in this book, the hospitals' predicament creates opportunities for the astute health care marketer.

On the physician side, the number of medical practices with managed care contracts jumped 34 percent in 1993, to 89 percent of all medical practices. In fact, managed care contracts generated a larger share of total revenues for medical practices in 1993 than 1992, with 20 percent of all revenues for practices coming from managed care contracts in 1993 versus 17 percent the year before.[28]

However, the growth of managed care has created both winners and losers in the physician world, particularly as a function of reliance upon the primary care "gatekeeper"–the health professional each patient must see before gaining access to specialists and certain types of inpatient admissions. Managed care plans have come to rely on gatekeepers and reward them accordingly. In survey data released in 1994, the Medical Group Management Association found that family practice physicians' annual income in 1993 varied from $119,000 in group practices with no managed care to $123,800 for those practices with more than 50 percent managed care clients. Effectively, physicians are being paid for their gatekeeping responsibilities.[29]

According to the MGMA survey, the annual income for several specialties dropped significantly when managed care was instituted. For example, invasive cardiology income dropped over $300,000 at practices without managed care to $242,000 at practices with more than 50 percent managed care clients; general surgery income dropped from $201,000 to $190,000; and orthopedic surgery dropped from $328,000 to $248,000.[30] MGMA's findings are confirmed by *Medical Economics Continuing Survey* which found that "family practitioners were the biggest winners with a 14.8 percent gain in median gross revenue . . . surgical specialists' median net dropped by $26,550, or 12.4 percent overall. . . . orthopedists lost approximately $13,000 and general surgeons nearly $23,000."[31]

In an environment where managed care is growing, specialists have other concerns as well, as their anxiety levels have been heightened by several recent projections of lower demand. Jonathan Weiner, for example, in the *Journal of the American Medical Association*, postulates that by the year 2000, there will be a surplus of 165,000 physicians, the majority of which will be specialists who will outstrip requirements by more than 60 percent.[32]

From a business, ownership, and insurance perspective, physicians historically have not played an active role in managed care. Consider, for example, that physicians, physician medical groups, and physician/hospital organizations (PHOs) combined, own only 7.5 percent of HMOs and 8.9 percent of Preferred Provider Organizations.[33]

This is somewhat curious, as physician "clout," particularly within a managed care/gatekeeper environment, is quite significant. Table 1.1 expresses the clout of primary care physicians aggregated into strategic alliances or networks; it is based upon the following assumptions:

- Each primary care physician has a base of 2,000 patients.
- Each primary care physician "controls" $100 per member per month in insurance premium revenues.
- Given 2,000 patients, each primary care physician will "control" about $640,000 per year in inpatient admissions.

TABLE 1.1. The Growing Clout of Primary Care Physicians

# PCPs	Patients	Insurance Premium $ Represented @ $100 PMPM	Hospital Inpatient $ Represented @ $640k/PCP/year
30	60,000	$ 72,000,000	$19,200,000
50	100,000	$120,000,000	$32,000,000
75	150,000	$180,000,000	$48,000,000
100	200,000	$240,000,000	$64,000,000

The growing clout of PCPs is of critical importance to the payer, medical delivery, and health care system marketer, as the ability to deliver an insured product increasingly lies in direct proportion to the number of PCPs in the delivery system. Consequently, a key role for the marketer within a growing managed care environment is recruiting primary care physicians. According to the *1994 Physician Recruitment Practice Survey* sponsored by Cejika & Co. and *Modern Healthcare*, 63 percent of hospitals surveyed indicated that they recruited family practice physicians in 1993, up from 25 percent in the previous year, and 78 percent of the respondents indicated that they were planning to recruit FPs in 1994.[34]

The evolution of managed care has also created a change in the patterns of provider reimbursement which is of critical importance for the marketer. In particular, on an ever increasing basis, financial risk is being moved away from the payer to the provider, creating new product opportunities and a significant increase in the need for marketing input.

As shown in Table 1.2, provider reimbursement has evolved from fee for service (FFS) and cost plus, through per diems and FFS with withholds, to the Relative Value Resource Based System (RVRBS), to capitation in many different forms, up to global capitation.

For example, physicians as a group are capitated for all professional services (fee for service with a 20 percent withhold) and are responsible for a percentage of hospital cost variance from budget. Hospitals are paid DRGs (Diagnostic Related Groups) by Preferred Care, a 160,000 member IPA in upstate New York. Freedom Health

TABLE 1.2. Patterns of Provider Reimbursement

Fee for Service
Discounted Fee for Service
Global Pricing
Case Rates
Incentives
Budgets
Withholds
Specialty Carve-outs
Partial Capitation
Global Capitation

Care in Wayne, Pennsylvania capitates primary care physicians, pays hospitals a per diem, and pays specialists on a fee-for-service basis with withhold. HMO Pennsylvania, an 800,000 member HMO owned by U.S. Healthcare, capitates PCPs with a withhold, pays most specialists on a fee-for- service basis with no withhold (some specialties are capitated), and pays hospitals on a per diem basis. However, PCPs in this system are at risk individually for specialist care.

The shift of risk toward providers has significant implications for the payer, medical delivery, and health care system marketer, particularly in terms of product development. *Who* takes risk will be an important determinant in the composition, positioning, and marketing of the medical delivery system. For example, certain managed care products of the Community Mutual Insurance Corporation in Cincinnati, Ohio have a limited panel: that is, a smaller subset of their entire panel of providers who have agreed to a risk-based reimbursement system different from their fellow providers.

How much risk providers are willing to accept may become a key determinant of product pricing, in the sense that the combination of full capitation and good negotiating on the part of payers may create additional margin which can be passed on to consumers in the form of lower premiums. For example, in Sullivan County, New York, one payer offered a physician's group a full capitation rate equal to

74 percent of premium. This means that these physicians are at full risk for all of the medical needs of their patient base, while the HMO takes $.26 of every premium dollar.

On the average, 82.5 percent of the HMO's premium dollar goes for medical costs and 12.3 percent for administrative costs, leaving 5.2 percent as operating income margin.[35] In the case of Sullivan County, the HMO's ability to negotiate at 74 percent of premium will produce excess margin (let's say about 6 to 8 percent), which in turn can be applied to reducing premium and consequently, producing a more competitive product. At a premium of $150 per month for single and $400 per month for family coverage, this excess margin can reduce single coverage premium costs by up to $144 per year, and family premium costs by over $380 per year.

Finally, *willingness to take risk* is an important component of the marketer's domain because the managed care organization offering risk must make the degree of risk acceptable to the risk-bearing entity. In other words, risk can be a factor contributing to the marketability of securing participation. Consider, for example, a Sullivan County scenario where a different payer enters the picture offering a capitation rate at 80 percent of premium.

Willingness to take risk works from the opposite end of the spectrum as well. Providers organized into a network can make their risk-willingness a key point of their marketing strategy, both as a basis for differentiation and enthusiasm for contributing to the ultimate marketability of a product to employers and consumers.

There has also been an evolution in provider incentives as a consequence of managed care. Hospitals, for example, in a non-managed care environment have incentives for high occupancy, high charges, and high utilization. The greater the evolution of managed care in the market, the greater the incentives are for reducing admissions and stays, and controlling costs.

Physicians in an non-managed care environment are motivated by patient volume and procedure, as their income opportunities are a direct function of how much or many services they can provide per patient. In an evolving managed care environment, physician incentives change with pressures for cost control, medical management, and capitation. Evolution in this sense moves the physician toward business, as well as clinical management of their practice, as the demand for better outcomes for less cost increases.

Marketing implications of this evolution for providers lies in their ability to "package" their product to managed care organizations. Both physicians and hospitals who demonstrate (and communicate) a willingness or an ability to work within the cost and quality demands of the market can significantly enhance their marketability. Correspondingly, the marketer's job becomes one of communicating this willingness and, in the process, differentiating their organization from others competing for a spot on the managed care organization's roster.

Marketing implications for payers may very well lie in their ability to help providers through the evolutionary process, with a strategic goal of creating a strong bond which can be leveraged for purposes of creating new products or services while concurrently creating opportunities for achieving competitive advantage. Consequently, a critical marketing consideration for the health care system as well as the integrated delivery network (IDN) centers around the issue of developing and sustaining physician loyalty and, in particular, PCP loyalty. The importance of this consideration is dramatic in the changing dynamic, because relationships are in transition. Consider, for example, that just as IDNs need not be exclusive to a payer, physicians need not be exclusive to an IDN. Consequently, physician bonding or relations programs must be an important part of any system's marketing and customer service program. These can include such activities as participation in policy making bodies, providing discounted administrative services, training and education programs, assistance in practice management (particularly from an information/MIS perspective), or even some forms of equity participation.

For example, in early 1993 Stephen Wiggins, CEO of Oxford Health Plan, developed the concept of "Private Practice Partnerships" (PPP) as a way to help physicians deal with the changing health care environment while at the same time, creating a win situation for patients and the HMO.[36]

PPPs are loosely affiliated groups of about twenty-five doctors without formal contractual relationships, organized to encourage physicians to collaborate for improved efficiency and quality. Although not mandatory, physicians who elect to participate get administrative help from Oxford and an opportunity to increase their earnings through a shared risk compensation plan. Oxford provides detailed staff, services, and clinical and financial information to the PPP, helping participants maintain their autonomy, gain information services and guidance, and empowerment. By the end of 1995, Oxford anticipates formulation of some sixty PPPs (with an original objective of forty), representing about 1,100 PCPs and 500 specialists.[37]

By promoting information sharing and consultation, patients benefit from greater access; and the streamlined management of physician's offices allows for better focus on patient needs. According to Dave Snow, Oxford's executive vice president, "physicians have really embraced the concept. . . . The combination of satisfied physicians delivering the best quality translates into healthy, satisfied patients–the ultimate goal of any HMO."[38]

INTEGRATION

The war in the health care industry, while driven by managed care, extends to organizational development and structures. Over the past thirty years, participants in the industry, particularly on the medical delivery side, have created organizational structures ranging from stand-alone efforts to horizontal integration to current trends of vertical integration. As these structures have evolved, so too has the role and responsibility of the health care system marketer.

The current trend, which is expected to continue into the foreseeable future, centers around the creation of *vertically integrated delivery systems or networks (IDN)*–a concept whose definition is changing rapidly and will continue to change over time. Table 1.3 lists characteristics of an IDN, leaving the inference that these entities are mainly medical delivery vehicles. However, some industry analysts maintain that IDNs include insurance and reinsurance, administrative, marketing, utilization management, and quality assurance components,[39] creating the opportunity for structuring many different types of IDNs as shown in Table 1.4. Many health benefit managers and policy specialists believe that well-structured inte-

TABLE 1.3. IDN Characteristics

* Combination of inpatient and outpatient services organized under one entity
* Operational at local or regional level
* Provides continuum of care from cradle to grave
* Contracts with HMOs or other payers
* Medical care delivered as a team
* Accepts financial risk
* Sharing of high technology equipment
* Increased emphasis on community health

grated networks will gain economies of scale, reduce redundant services, move toward eliminating unnecessary and inappropriate care and drive out poor quality health plans.[40]

The process of creating an IDN is intensely complex and sophisticated, requiring a combination of strategic, financial, administrative, operational, marketing, actuarial, and legal input. From a strategic perspective all three participants–physicians, hospitals, and payers–face a set of internal and external decisions. Physicians must assess whether to contract alone, or to form some type of entity like an IPA or MSO that will serve as their contracting mechanism, or to participate within the structure of provider organizations to which they belong. Hospitals, too, face the "go it alone" or "create a system/network" decision, and payers must decide what type of products (commercial, Medicare, Medicaid) will be included in an IDN mechanism. Once these internal decisions have been made, each participant faces a set of external strategic decisions, namely, selection of which participants with whom the IDN will be created.

For example, a network of primary care physicians can create an IDN with a tertiary hospital and an HMO to serve Medicaid recipients. Or, an IPA can contract with community hospitals, an academic medical, and an HMO to create an IDN serving a commercial population. Or, a network of specialists plus independent primary

TABLE 1.4. Creating an Integrated Delivery Network

Physicians
- Primary care
- Specialists
- Single specialty group
- Multi-specialty group
- Primary care network
- Specialist network
- Primary care/specialist network
- Medical staff
- PPO
- IPA
- ANY COMBINATION OF THE ABOVE

=

MEDICAL DELIVERY SYSTEM

+

Hospital
- Community hospital
- Tertiary hospital
- Academic medical center
- Hospital network
- Hospital system
- ANY COMBINATION OF THE ABOVE

+

Payers
- Commercial HMO
- Medicaid HMO
- Academic medical center
- Hospital network
- Hospital system
- ANY COMBINATION OF THE ABOVE

=

INTEGRATED DELIVERY NETWORK

care physicians plus a hospital network can create a medical delivery system to serve an HMO's Medicare membership.

Consider this: given ten types of physician entities, five types of hospital entities, and the number of possible payer product combinations, in any given market, virtually millions of different IDN configurations can be created!

While IDNs represent an opportunistic way to bring managed care into a market, there are a variety of other factors stimulating their role on the health care battlefield: the expansion of managed care, employer interest in working with small networks, rising payer discounts, decreasing margins and flat income growth, geographic and target market expansion opportunities, new product opportunities, an increasing demand for capital investment, community benefit demands, and growing overhead, to name a few.

However, perhaps the dominant motivational influences driving providers to evolve into IDNs are fear and confusion, born out of financial self-interest and institutional survival instincts. These influences represent dramatic and compelling tools for the marketer with responsibilities for organizing an IDN, as being able to position and sell the IDN concept to participants on the basis of security represents an overwhelmingly powerful marketing platform.

Of over 1,100 hospitals and forty health systems responding to a joint survey conducted by Deloitte and Touche and *Hospitals and Health Networks*, 24 percent indicate that they already belong to an integrated delivery system; 71 percent say that they either belong to or are developing an IDS. Further, 67 percent said that it is necessary for an acute care hospital to have some form of Physician/Hospital Organization (PHO).[41]

According to an article in *Group Practice Managed Healthcare News*, by the end of 1992, about one-quarter of U.S. hospitals had an existing PHO or one under development.[42] In another recent study (*Physician-Hospital Organizations: Profile 1995*), Ernst and Young found that forty-one states now have PHOs, with more than half of these PHOs less than a year old and nearly 75 percent under 25 months.[43]

However, it is not just hospitals that are charging into vertical integration. Physicians too are forming physician-only networks, on both single and multispecialty basis, as well as increasingly organizing into groups. Consider, for example, that between 1965 and 1991, the number of physicians practicing in groups grew from 28,000 to 184,000, and the number of group practices grew by 286 percent (4,300 to 16,600).[44]

Citing statistics from the forthcoming *Marion Merrell Dow Managed Care Digest*, the Medical Group Management Association writes that while medical practices are fully participating in managed care, few have ventured toward integration:

> In selected indicators of integrated health systems, only two areas applied to the majority of medical practices: most practice physicians (95 percent) have hospital staff privileges and more than half (52 percent) practice as independent contractors. Any real attempts at integration are rare. Only 9 percent of medical practices participate in a joint venture with a hospital. Less than 3 percent of medical practices are involved in other arrangements such as a management services organization or clinic without walls.[45]

For the medical delivery marketer, the evolution of integrated delivery networks has both *internal* and *external* implications.

Internally, the medical delivery marketer can and should have both strategic and operational responsibilities. Strategically, selection of the type of IDN most appropriate for the organization should be a function of the medical delivery marketer's assessment of market dynamics and opportunities. The operation, development, launch, and ultimately the success of the IDN will require packaging and selling the concept to prospect/participants. Both of these responsibilities are discussed further in Chapter 3.

Externally, once the IDN is developed, the marketer's responsibilities must be oriented to "selling" the IDN; that is, securing contracts. One target, of course, is HMOs. Ernst and Young's *Profile* reports that PHO contracts with Preferred Provider Organizations (PPOs) account for 41 percent of PHO covered lives, and that 52 percent of PHOs have contracts with HMOs, accounting for 18 percent of covered lives. However, 72 percent of PHO officials surveyed hope for or are planning on HMO contracts.[46]

Integrated Delivery Networks also have opportunities to sell directly to employers in competition with indemnity insurers and managed care organizations. If networks offer a favorable premium rate, businesses certainly will be interested, particularly self-funded ERISA exempt corporations.[47] Thus, the marketer's responsibility must be to assess the entire local market for opportunities and to evaluate the consequences of securing those opportunities.

Another implication of this evolution for the marketer lies in the fact that the IDN may increasingly represent a means for product differentiation. In other words, the composition of the medical delivery participants within the health care system (in concert with appropriate marketing communications activities) can be used to create both tangible and perceptual differences for influencing purchasers' buying behaviors.

It can be reasonably argued that the greater the degree of managed care penetration in a market, the more likely it will be that differentiation based around medical benefits will play a smaller role in marketing strategies, as the ability to duplicate any competitive advantages accruing from such a strategic move will be short-lived in nature. For example, in markets where managed care penetration is low, positioning against indemnity plans has traditionally been a function of leveraging cost and benefit advantages (while minimizing access restrictions).

In markets of high managed care penetration, using benefits as a marketing tool led to "benefit wars," where product innovations were quickly brought to market and then duplicated by competitors, such that any advantage initiated by the innovating organization was quickly negated. For example, in many markets free well-baby visits were used by HMOs as a means of differentiation from both indemnity and HMO competitors. While those HMOs who brought this benefit to market first did accrue a competitive advantage, such advantage was short-lived as their competition duplicated the maneuver in short order.

If differentiation around benefits is not a viable strategic option as the market matures from a managed care perspective, then a health care system is left with brand identity, cost, access, and quality as differentiating variables. It can therefore be reasonably expected that who participates in the system and the quality of their participation will become key tools in the marketer's positioning, packaging, and promotion environment of the future. System A, for example, will compete against System B around the fact that it includes Hospitals X, Y, and Z and the Top 25 percent of providers in the market "as measured by customer outcomes and satisfaction."

Integration, however, does not come cheaply and many efforts to integrate fall apart at the capitalization stage where the realities of consultant, legal, and MIS fees meet the intentions of IDN organizers. According to the Advisory Board, a Washington, DC-based health care think tank, start-up costs for a 100 physician foundation, staff, or equity plan generally range from $8 million to $30 million.[48] However, the Board estimates that doctors could form a physician/hospital organization for as little as $50,000, or a group practice without walls for about $100,000.

Basically speaking, the tighter the network, the higher the cost to develop and operate. Table 1.5, taken from *AMA News*, provides a comparative assessment of costs for building an integrated entity consisting of 100 physicians.

CONSOLIDATIONS AND MERGERS

Another major force driving the war in the health care industry as a consequence of managed care is the consolidation, merger, and acquisition activity occurring between and among payers, physicians, and hospitals. Virtually every form of economic venture characterizes the health industry marketplace. Start-ups, mergers, acquisitions, strategic agreements, joint ventures, coalitions, and so on are proliferating everywhere.[49]

The *Deloitte and Touche/HH&N Survey* found that a majority of respondents think that their hospitals will not be operating as standalone facilities in five years. It was this recognition, for example, that prompted officials at Lake City Medical Center in Florida to pursue strategic relationships with other hospitals, like their affiliation with Shands Hospitals, allowing Lake City to concentrate on providing primary care and some specialty services to its community as well as access to Shand's tertiary level of care. Executives at Lake City also saw the need to affiliate with St. Vincent's Medical Center in Jacksonville because their location less than 60 miles

TABLE 1.5. Integration Costs

	Start-up Costs	Key Expenses	Annual Operating Costs	How Recovered
Service Bureau	$10,000 to $25,000	Billing, software, set up administration	$500,000 to $1 million: staff system, operating costs	Physician service fees
Group Practice Without Walls	$100,000 to $1 million	Set up administration, software, hardware for physicians	$500,000 to $1 million: staff, administration	Physician service fees
Open PHO	$50,000 to $150,000	Staff education, writing professional services agreements	$150,000 to $1 million: staff, claims processing, other system costs	Physician membership fees
Closed PHO	$200,000 to $1 million	Staff education, designing membership application and selection, professional services agreements	$200,000 to $1.5 million: staff, claims processing, membership selection, other system costs	Physician membership fees

TABLE 1.5. (continued)

	Start-up Costs	Key Expenses	Annual Operating Costs	How Recovered
Asset MSO	$1 million to $4 million	Purchase of hard assets, legal fees	$11 million to $14 million: staff, practice administration	Physician fees
Foundation	$10 million to $30 million	Purchase of hard assets, intangibles and accounts receivable, legal fees	$23.5 to $29 million: staff, practice administration, physician salary and benefits	Revenue from physician practices
Staff Model	$10 million to $16 million	Purchase or start-up of practices	Practice administration, physician salary and benefits	Revenue from physician practices
Equity Model	$8 million to $10 million	Purchase or start-up of practices	Practice administration, physician salary and benefits	Revenue from physician practices

from seven tertiary giants left them with no option but to affiliate in order to ensure their survival as a suburban hospital.[50]

Merger and acquisition frenzy is also taking place within the Health Maintenance Organization universe. HMOs with strong regional presence are merging with one another or acquiring smaller companies in order to gain market share and negotiating clout with providers.[51] According to *Hospitals and Health Networks*:

> Among the issues that will face the rapidly changing HMO industry are: tensions between size and efficiency/market-responsiveness; the potential for various health care reform scenarios to affect enrollment patterns and market planning; potential differences in approaches open to for-profit and not-for-profit managed care companies; and the future viability of different structural models of managed care organizations.[52]

Merger and acquisition activity is being conducted at both local/regional and national levels. For example:

- In Seattle, Washington, Virginia Mason Medical Center (one hospital, fourteen clinic locations, $301 million net revenues, and a 45,000 member health plan) and Group Health Cooperative of Puget Sound (an HMO with 483,000 members, net revenues of $931 million, and ownership of two hospitals, thirty primary care medical centers, and five specialty centers), created an alliance to develop an expanded delivery system and to initially develop and market joint insurance products.
- In Chicago, an academic medical center (Rush-Presbyterian-St. Luke's Medical Center) and a national insurance company (Prudential Insurance Company of America) merged their Chicago-based managed care operations to create Rush Prudential Health Plans, marketing three managed care plans in seven counties in Illinois and Indiana.
- In Detroit, the Henry Ford Health System (six hospitals, thirty-seven ambulatory care centers, two nursing homes, 450,000 member HMO) joined forces with Mercy Health Services and Blue Cross/Blue Shield of Michigan to form a mega-network.

- In Boston, Brigham and Women's Hospital and Massachusetts General Hospital merged to create a faculty of 2,200 doctors and 2,900 residents to improve care, to reduce costs, and for purposes of forming additional alliances with community hospitals and managed care programs.
- In 1994, Merck & Co. spent $6.6 billion to acquire Medco Containment Services, SmithKline Beecham bought Diversified Pharmaceutical Services, and Eli Lilly purchased PCS Health Systems–all in order to integrate distribution.
- WellPoint Health Networks, Inc. (owned 80 percent by Blue Cross of California) and Health Systems International Inc. (HSI) created the nation's largest publicly traded health care network with 2.2 million HMO members in seven states and 3 million PPO members in 34 states. This merger came on the heels of a failed $1.5 billion bid by Foundation Health Plan to acquire HSI.

One of the more fascinating stories paralleling the evolutionary trend of mergers and acquisitions is that of the Columbia/HCA Corporation. Lindy Richardson, a Senior Vice President at Columbia/HCA, maintains that the key factor to marketplace success in health care right now is price, with quality becoming the major issue in two to three years. She stresses that Columbia/HCA believes that all health care providers must provide comprehensive one-stop shopping health care to customers, and that "in the next generation of health care, you see the hospital industry, the provider, the facilities, the physicians, employer groups and insurance companies dividing themselves into two categories–'those who get it' and 'those who don't'."[53]

According to Susanne Robbins, a Vice President for Network Development, the company's success is built upon four foundations: "(1) We build local and regional healthcare delivery systems; (2) we have a one-stop medical shopping approach; (3) we have the highest quality most cost-effective programs available on a market-by-market basis; and (4) we make it so easy to do business with you, you won't want to go anywhere else."[54]

INFORMATION AND INFORMATION
TECHNOLOGY

Marketers in the health care industry are increasingly learning that information can be a very powerful tool for understanding and managing the health care battlefield. Cost, quality, outcomes, and patient satisfaction are increasingly becoming key elements in health care plan (and system) marketing and communications efforts as, to a large degree, competitive pressures are increasing information requirements. Sophisticated buyers of health care are demanding access to cost and utilization data about their employees, as well as statistical parameters of health care plan performance pursuant to their making purchase decisions. Information–and the appropriate packaging and communication of that information–becomes a tool in the hands of the astute health care marketer.

As markets have been increasingly penetrated by managed care, information needs of payers, providers, and users have shifted from claims payment and billing to cost containment to cost containment through quality care. While large employers and others who are financing health care are demanding data on patient satisfaction and outcomes, at the same time, changing medical delivery systems into vertically integrated networks of HMOs, hospitals, physicians, and other medical providers and health plans is no longer an alternative for the future–it has become a business necessity.[55]

Prefatory to building a health care system and in order to acquire managed care contracts, providers will need to ensure and demonstrate that they have capture, storage, and analytic capabilities relative to costs of care, reimbursement, practice patterns, and clinical outcomes. Once a contract (i.e., customer) is obtained, the information system will need to ensure and demonstrate real-time access, confidentiality of clinical data, the ability to meet customer expectations, capitation management capabilities, and the ability to share clinical and administrative information. In effect, the quality and capabilities of the information system become marketing tools for acquiring and sustaining managed care contracts.

In addition to improving business management functions, information and information technology have other implications for the payer, medical delivery, and health care system marketer in terms of product pricing and promotion. For example, the Orlando Health Care Group (OHCG) made an investment of $750,000 to develop an information system that, according to a study performed by Arthur D. Little, is expected to generate over $1.5 million in annual cost savings (once fully implemented) from improvements in time management alone.[56] The $8.11 per member savings that OHGC will realize, from the marketer's perspective, represents an opportunity to pass along savings to their customers, which in turn enhances OGHC's competitive position. (On the other hand, the $8.11 per member represents additional margin which could also be passed along to its owners.)

Through the eyes of a marketer, OGHC's system can be viewed from the perspective of feature and benefits, which can be used in marketing communications activities for purposes of differentiation and competitive advantage (see Figure 1.2). Consider, for example, collateral materials telling OGHC's customers (i.e., managed care organizations, employers, etc.) about its system's capabilities and how those capabilities benefit the customer. Until such time that OGHC's competitors can duplicate its information systems and technology, their competitive advantages are significant in terms of driving preference. Combined with lower service costs, perhaps expressed in lower per member per month capitation rates, the OGHC "product" would represent a formidable foe.

This is not to say, however, that the state of information technology and systems in the integrated health care environment has become a reality, as growing industry complexities are creating a demand for entirely new information systems and infrastructures. Currently, information infrastructures are inadequate to support demands and there is an appalling lack of standardization. While the opportunity may be here, needed data is unavailable because it either doesn't exist or because it is held within multiple, incompatible systems. With the lack of standardization, data that is accessible can be unusable due to an absence of data definitions and coding standards.[57]

Clinical data, too, has entered the world of information technology. For example, Alcatel Network Systems, along with Lambert Communications, EMC Corporation, and other companies recently launched HealthNet 2000—a system described as the first digital,

FIGURE 1.2. Information Systems as a Marketing Tool

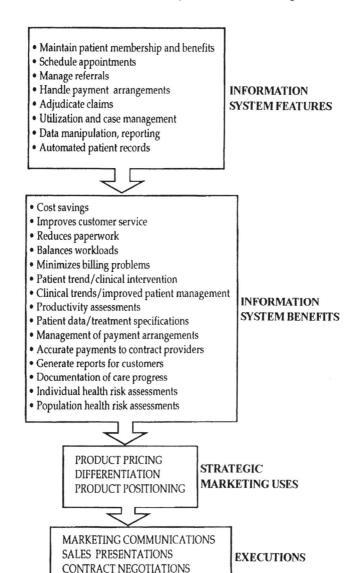

interactive, video-on-demand network for hospitals, managed care companies, and other health care related organizations. According to Rebecca Lambert, CEO of Lambert Communications, HealthNet 2000 will "allow hospitals to talk to each other, and will provide educational programming for healthcare professionals and patients alike."[58]

From the health care system's marketer perspective, the ability to electronically network the medical delivery system is quite exciting. A provider no longer needs to be located in a local market in order to be part of the delivery system. Thus, a health care system in Phoenix, Arizona can include The Cleveland Clinic in Cleveland, Ohio on its panel of providers. It is not unreasonable to see the establishment of long distance clinical relationships as a reality in the near future, representing some wonderful opportunities for positioning the health care system's access and quality–"Now you can see the world's best heart specialists without ever leaving Phoenix. . . ."

In addition to the infrastructure and clinical issues discussed above, the payer, medical delivery, and health care system marketer now has access to information in a way previously impossible. Electronic databases, such as those offered by HCIA of Baltimore, Maryland, for example, are full of information about individual hospitals and health maintenance organizations which can be used for market and competitive analysis. Trade organizations such as Group Health Association of America and the Medical Group Management Association now offer on-line services, where the marketer cannot only get industry news and trend information, but also can access articles and reference materials. We have used these databases and on-line services for efforts ranging from identification of market entry opportunities to assessments of financial strengths and weaknesses of competitors in specific markets.

Finally, with the ability to store, process, and manipulate large quantities of information right from a desktop, the health care marketer can engage in *database marketing*, where specific needs of specific sets of customers can be identified, leading to the creation of dedicated programs or services. For example, for purposes of customer relations and retention, the marketer can identify families with first child newborns, and deliver programs on parenting skills for new patients. Or, through querying disenrollees, the marketer can build a database which not only provides information on reasons for disenrollment, but also, establishes the ground for building a dialogue with the disenrolle which can turn them back into a customer.

GOVERNMENT PROGRAMS

In the changing dynamic, some of the bloodiest battles between payer and provider will be fought on the battlefield of government programs–Medicaid and Medicare. Where the elderly and poor were once considered risky, from health and financial perspectives, legislative change at federal and state levels are creating an unprecedented opportunity for financial gain for payers, and to a lesser extent, providers as a consequence of initiatives to encourage government program eligible to move into managed care.

Medicaid

Long considered pariahs by the health insurance industry and system, the poor are increasingly becoming a valuable commodity as state governments, battered by soaring Medicaid budgets, are rushing to move welfare recipients into managed care programs.[59] As reported in *The Wall Street Journal*, "HMOs that until recently shunned the poor now see those eligible for Medicaid as a major source of enrollment growth (and) profits. By providing Medicaid patients with their own primary care doctors, HMOs believe they can sharply curtail the use of high cost emergency rooms for routine care and rein in surging costs, while vastly improving health care for the poor and better managing chronic diseases such as diabetes and asthma."

Administered by the states, Medicaid is financed jointly by the states and the federal government. Since its inception in the mid-1960s under Title XIX of the Social Security Act, the Medicaid program has experienced dramatic growth in beneficiaries and expenditures to the point where today, significant changes in the way the program is operated and administered are receiving priority consideration by Congress and the Clinton Administration. The federal contribution–ranging from 50 to 78 percent–is based upon a state's per capita income.[60] At is inception in 1966, federal payments for the Medicaid program were about $800 million for some 11 million recipients. Currently, the number of Medicaid beneficiaries has grown to 36 million and according to the Congressional Budget Office, federal payments in 1995 will reach $90 billion (57 percent) and state payments will reach $68 billion (43 percent), accounting for the program's nearly $160 billion price tag.[61]

Growth in Medicaid spending has exceeded growth in beneficiaries, with program costs usually increasing by well over 10 percent annually. Between 1988 and 1992 alone, Medicaid spending *doubled*, and in 1993, Medicaid comprised over 5 percent of total federal spending, 39 percent of federal aid to state and local governments, and 13 percent of total national health expenditures.[62] The Congressional Budget Office estimates that the program will continue to grow by an average of more than 10 percent annually for the foreseeable future, accounting for an increasingly larger share of total federal spending.[63]

Beginning in 1983, and rapidly accelerating over the past several years, state governments have sought to slow the increase in costs through various managed Medicaid programs under waivers from current federal legislation, with approval from the federal government's Health Care Financing Administration (HCFA). In fact, states are increasingly relying on managed care arrangements as their primary strategy to improve access to care for poor children and non-disabled adults and to reduce Medicaid expenditures. Changes in federal Medicaid requirements on the use of managed care and the growth of managed care in the private sector have contributed to the recent dramatic increase in Medicaid managed care enrollment. Even in the absence of federal legislation, as states continue to struggle to improve access and restrain costs, the shift from fee-for-service to managed care for Medicaid will likely continue.[64]

Currently, of the nearly 36 million eligible Medicaid recipients, approximately 7.8 million eligibles (23 percent) are receiving care through HMOs and similar plans, representing a 63 percent increase in enrollment over 1994, and up from just 14 percent in 1993.[65] As shown in Figure 1.3, considering that only 750,000 beneficiaries

FIGURE 1.3. Growth in Managed Medicaid Enrollment, 1983-1994

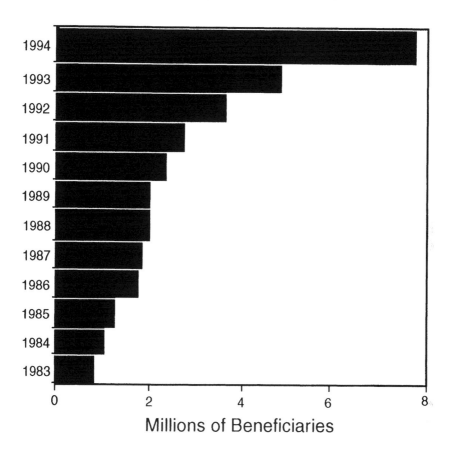

Millions of Beneficiaries

were enrolled in managed care in 1983, managed Medicaid growth has been significant.

The rise in costs and numbers of Medicaid recipients combined with a conservative Congress and pressures to balance the budget, has made the Medicaid program a target for federal legislators. Perhaps the greatest and most significant impact faced by providers responding to these changes is the likelihood that under the Medicaid program of the future, organizations will need to do more with less. While as of this writing specific program details have not been fixed, all current Congressional initiatives have two common themes: slowing the growth of spending via a cap on annual expenditures; and passing funds to states on a block grant basis. Impacts of these initiatives include:

- less Medicaid dollars available, which under current legislative proposals amount to up to $160 billion by 2002;
- the possibility of reduced fees for providers;
- pressures to reduce costs effected through reductions in inpatient admissions, use of emergency rooms, and lengths of stay;
- shifts from costly institutional services to lower priced ambulatory services;
- the possibility that fewer current recipients will remain Medicaid eligible as states obtain authority to make revisions in eligibility requirements;
- the possibility that losses in hospital and physician income would be made up by *cost shifting*, or changing higher rates to patients in the private sector.

The net effect of these changes will be to move more and more Medicaid eligibles into managed care at an ever increasing, accelerated rate, as short of draconian expenditure reductions or revisions to eligibility requirements, managed care is perhaps the only means for absorbing the financial impacts of federal and state initiatives. Consequently, opportunities for managed Medicaid are staggering from the health care marketer's perspective. Assuming an average per member per month capitation of $150, the 26.2 million eligibles not enrolled in managed care, alone, represent over $40 *billion* in revenue across the nation.

In the changing dynamic, payers, hospitals, and physicians will wage a fierce battle over Medicaid eligibles. At the health care system level, battles for enrollment are currently being waged, and will only intensify over the next several years. Consider, for example, that in New York City alone there are currently some eighteen HMOs competing for Medicaid eligibles.

The marketing battle for Medicaid eligibles is challenging and complex. As a consequence of fraudulent marketing practices during the 1970s and 1980s, most states have severely restricted the ability of HMOs to market directly to Medicaid eligibles.

For example, Fidelis Care, a managed Medicaid plan launched

by Catholic Medical Center in New York City (Brooklyn and Queens) found the marketing process to be quite challenging. Physician recruitment was not an issue in this case, as staff physicians from the hospital and their free-standing health centers were tapped to deliver medical services. According to June Stollman, CEO of Healthscope/United who helped develop and now manages Fidelis Care, "Our job was to access a multi-ethnic population speaking different languages, responding to different marketing incentives, in an area of high unemployment and poor health, who have traditionally accessed health care at the emergency rooms of their local hospitals, usually at the late stages of illness."[66]

Fidelis' marketing approach included neighborhood-level marketing using language-adept representatives living in the catchment area; a communications program consisting of posters, multi-language brochures, member handbooks, promotional items, an informational video, and paid advertising (radio and outdoor); and a strong, language-adept member services program aimed at educating new members on how to use the system. Since its opening in October of 1993, membership has reached 15,000, and by 1996, is expected to reach 30,000.

However, providers–in particular hospitals that heavily depend upon Medicaid revenues–face another battle: survival. For many provider organizations, Medicaid represents conflicting objectives. On the one hand, the organization's mission or charter may include community service values that require the organization to serve the poor. On the other hand, even though Medicaid reimbursement still represents cash flow for the organization, the financial implications of serving a Medicaid population are becoming increasingly more severe. Finding a balance between community service and financial impacts will be difficult for many provider organizations.

Faced with the potential loss of revenues from both revisions to eligibility requirements and changes in utilization under managed Medicaid, many hospitals will need to seek and implement strategies to recapture revenue shortfalls. Strategies might include increasing volume in terms of increasing market share; and/or shifting costs to private payers; and/or developing an integrated organization that maximizes the ability to retain the total flow of dollars and any utilization savings.

Medicare

The Medicare program was established in 1965 to provide health insurance and economic security to elderly Americans. By 1967, Medicare served 19 million enrollees at a cost of $4.2 billion. Today, some 37 million Americans have Medicare coverage (more than 97 percent of the elderly) at a cost of $175 billion, representing 11 percent of federal budget outlays and 20 percent of federal entitlement spending. By the year 2000, program expenditures are expected to exceed $285 billion.[67]

The federal government has supported enrollment of Medicare beneficiaries in HMOs since the early 1970s. Today, payments to HMOs are made either on a capitated risk basis, or based upon reasonable costs. Risk contracts place the health plan at full risk for the cost of providing Medicare benefits. Cost contracts are reimbursed on a reasonable cost basis. Today, nearly three quarters of all Medicare beneficiaries live in an area with a Medicare managed care plan available.[68]

Currently, there are about 3.1 million managed Medicare enrollees out of a prospect pool of some 37 million. Seniors have confounded conventional wisdom suggesting they would resist switching providers because HMOs are offering better coverage at less cost and with less paperwork burdens. Because cost cutting strategies would be politically unattractive and not serve the public health, enthusiasm is growing for shifting more Medicare patients into managed care arrangements as a way to reduce cash outlays without diminishing quality of care.[69]

While not as large as the managed Medicaid program, managed Medicare has experienced significant growth as shown in Figure 1.4. From 1994 to 1995 alone, enrollment increased by over 25 percent.

While the big numbers have been concentrated in areas with dense senior populations or high managed care penetration (the West and South Florida for example), Medicare-risk HMOs are quickly moving into key Sunbelt, Northeast, and Midwest markets. As a consequence, physician organizations and hospitals are increasingly assuming risk for this population under a capitated system which appears to offer providers the opportunity to better

FIGURE 1.4. Growth in Managed Medicare Enrollment

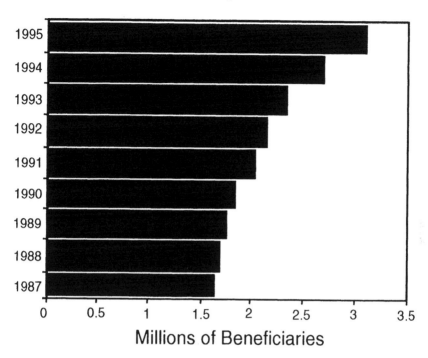

meet Medicare recipients' health needs while managing their care more effectively.[70] According to Peter Yedidia, president of Geriatric Health Systems, "Under Medicare fee-for-service reimbursement, services important to maintaining seniors' health are not reimbursed—including early risk identification, health promotion and case management, as well as many nonphysician practitioner interventions. Capitated financing, in contrast, supplies front end dollars and the flexibility for organizations to provide services that can better address older persons' health needs before debilitating and expensive crisis occur."[71]

The typical managed Medicare marketing process requires a three-fold approach: recruiting providers; enrolling members; and educating members on how, where, and when to access services. Now, marketers must sell direct to the end-user, requiring tools, techniques, and sales strategies significantly different than those used to penetrate the employer market. For example, some HMOs offer retirees dance tickets or a free meal in return for listening to a forty-five-minute sales pitch. Recruiters earn $60 or more for each member they enroll, and top salespeople say they sign up about 40 percent of those who hear a presentation.[72]

Employers who offer retirees health benefits also seem to be climbing aboard the managed Medicare bandwagon, as it offers opportunities to cut costs and reduce accounting charges under FAS 106. Nationally, 17 percent of employers offered at least one managed Medicaid plan to retirees in 1994, up from only 7 percent in 1993. According to Robin Weiner of the benefits consulting firm Foster Higgins, retirees' resistance to joining managed care plans out of fear of having to change doctors "isn't as big a problem as popularly thought, particularly in California where retirees are likely to find their long-time personal physicians included in their HMO's provider network."[73]

From the HMO's perspective, plans collect payment from the government at a rate equal to 95 percent of the average cost of treating Medicare patients in a given region. HMOs are free to pay doctors, hospitals, and other providers as they see fit, and if their cost of treating a patient is less than the government's contribution, they keep the difference.[74]

With the payment rate fixed and independent of both HMO costs and the competitiveness of the local managed care environment, payers compete only for the enrollment of Medicare beneficiaries, and consequently, efficient, low-cost HMOs may be able to offer more generous benefit packages to enrollees and still prosper under the fixed capitation rate.[75] In fact, research suggests that HMO costs in caring for their enrollees are at least 10 percent less than the government would have spent on fee-for-service care.[76]

Given these facts, it is no surprise that HMOs are rushing to bring a Medicare-risk product to market. Currently, over 150 HMOs contract with HCFA on a risk basis. From 1993 to 1994 there was a 21 percent increase in the number of contracts and the year 1994-1995 showed a 41 percent increase.[77]

Similar to Medicaid, the potential is staggering. At an average capitation rate of $450 PMPM, the 33 million Medicare beneficiaries not enrolled in a managed care plan represent billions and billions and billions of dollars of untapped revenue. Just by reducing utilization by $10 PMPM, a managed care plan with 20,000 enrollees can deliver $2.4 million right to the bottom line.

Consequently, the local-market battles between managed Medicare plans is intense, and will only become fiercer in the changing dynamic. Consider, for example, that over two-thirds of all plans currently offer beneficiaries health care coverage for no monthly premium, and that the majority of Medicaid enrollees incur little or no out-of-pocket expenses.[78] Further, many risk-based HMOs provide additional benefits, at no extra charge, above and beyond those covered by Medicare in an attempt to obtain enrollees.

The glee experienced by many HMOs as they ponder the possibilities of managed Medicare has been given a significant shot in the arm by the current Republican congress. Given the projected growth in expenditures, and the pressure to reduce the federal deficit, the Medicare program is being restructured. In particular, a key feature in Congress' plans to curb the growth in federal outlays in Medicare is to increase enrollment in managed care organizations. This shift is projected by the Congressional Budget Office to save about $30 billion to $50 billion through the year 2002, depending upon how reimbursement rates and incentives are structured.[79] In conjunction with reducing provider payments, increasing contributions from beneficiaries, and delivering care in more efficient and economical ways, expenditures for Medicare are anticipated to drop by tens of billions of dollars through the year 2000.

The marketing related elements of Medicare reform include offering eligibles more choice in health care plans, including traditional fee-for-service plans, HMOs, point-of-service plans, and high deductible plans with medical savings accounts. In the battle for market share in the changing dynamic, it is not unreasonable to expect that payers will offer a mix of these different products.

There are, however, storm clouds looming on the horizon for HMOs. First, as of the time of this writing, it is highly likely that there will be changes made to reimbursement methodologies. According to *Washington Health Week* (November 11, 1995), "Medicare capitated plans in countries with high payment rates will see tight growth caps and find it hard to continue offering additional benefits or reduced premiums. FFS plans would gain a competitive advantage in those areas, and HMO enrollment could go down. Conversely, low-paid counties would gradually see their capitation rates go up and attract managed care."

Second, on what may become one of the more intriguing battlefields in the changing dynamic, Federal Medicare reforms have created the ability of providers to organize and establish risk-based *Provider Sponsored Networks or Organizations* (PSNs) to specifically target an over-65 population. It is no secret that the brunt of negative financial impacts from Medicaid and Medicare reform will fall squarely on the shoulders of doctors and hospitals. According to some estimates, hospital losses may range up to $75 billion over a seven-year period, while estimated losses range from $35 billion to $60 billion for doctors, nursing homes, home health services, laboratories, and durable medical equipment suppliers.[80]

PSNs present the greatest opportunities for providers, and in particular integrated delivery networks, to recapture financial losses from cost cutting efforts. In effect, a PSN would accept total risk—both administrative and financial—for their Medicare enrollees while retaining any utilization savings. Concurrently, PSNs would assume responsibility for marketing and enrollment.

On the payer's side, the battle line will be drawn upon the map of their experience, capital reserves, awareness, management information systems, and strong lobbying presence in Washington and at state capitols. Providers will come to the battlefield at a disadvantage, lacking many of the characteristics that will make payers strong foes. However, they do possess one weapon that may so significantly outweigh any temporary fiscal (or other) payer advantages, that with strong strategic, financial, and marketing planning, they can not only win the battle, but perhaps the whole war over Medicare enrollment.

What's the "secret weapon"? . . . affinity. That is, the loyalty of their patients to their physician's practice. Within the next several years, I would expect to hear the following conversation in a physician's office:

Dr. Smith: Mr. and Mrs. Jones, what's your insurance coverage?
The Jones: Why, we're with The GoodHealth Plan . . . you know, the one with no premiums and no paperwork hassle.

Dr. Smith: I'm no longer accepting GoodHealth Plan so I want you to join MyPlan . . . it's exactly the same as what you have now..

The Jones: O.K.

Dr. Smith: See Sally on your way out and she'll sign you right up.

The battle between payer and provider over Medicare should produce some of the greatest fireworks and a continuing stream of casualties over the next several years. It is foolish to think, however, that HMOs will be sitting idly by, awaiting the demise of their Medicare business. It is reasonable to expect grand alliances between payers and providers over Medicare eligibles, some on a shared-risk basis, others characterized by HMOs serving in administrative capacities only.

OTHER TRENDS
IN THE CHANGING DYNAMIC

While the trends discussed above are perhaps the most significant for the health care system marketer, there are a number of other trends which must be recognized, including:

- A movement toward needs assessment and outcomes management on a community level
- Growth of the home health industry
- Creation of "lite" hospitals, designed for patient stays of only two to three days
- Continuing advances in medical technology and drug therapies
- Use of advanced statistical modeling tool to create products and forecast demand.

As will be discussed in the following chapters, managing or capitalizing upon these trends and others represent the basis for success in the changing dynamic. Marketers must not only be ahead of the curve in recognizing trends, but also be proactive in creating trends.

REFERENCE NOTES

1. Vincent P. Barabba and Gerald Zaltman, *Hearing the Voice of the Market: Competitive Advantage Through Creative Use of Market Information* (Boston, MA: Harvard Business School Press, 1991).

2. Ibid., p. 61.

3. Ibid., p. 162.

4. C. Wayne Higgins and Eugene D. Meyers, "The Economic Transformation of American Health Insurance: Implications for the Hospital Industry" in *Managed Care Strategies, Networks, and Management*, ed. Montague Brown (Gaithersburg, MD: Aspen Publishers, Inc., 1994), pp. 55-61.

5. G. Rodney Wolford, Montague Brown, and Barbara P. McCool, "Getting To Go in Managed Care" in *Managed Care Strategies, Networks, and Management*, pp. 3-16.

6. Myron D. Fottler and Donna Malvey, "Multiprovider Systems," in *Health Care Administration–Principles, Practices, Structure, and Delivery*, ed. Lawrence F. Wolper (Gaithersburg, MD: Aspen Publishers, Inc., 1995), pp. 489-515.

7. Ibid.

8. Ibid.

9. S.M. Shortell, "The Evolution of Hospital Systems: Unfilled Promises and Self-Fulfilling Prophesies" in *Medical Care Review*, Vol. 45, No. 20 (1988), pp. 177-214.

10. "Ask the Expert–Interview with John H. Eichert, President, Hastings Healthcare Group, Inc." in *The Alliance Bulletin* (Chicago, IL: Alliance for Healthcare Strategy and Marketing, February 1995), pp. 6-7.

11. G. Rodney Wolford, Montague Brown, and Barbara P. McCool, "Getting to Go in Managed Care."

12. "Ask the Expert," in *The Alliance Bulletin*, pp. 6-7.

13. For example, the early to mid-1980s saw the rise of Partners National Health Plans, a joint venture between Aetna and Voluntary Hospitals of America.

14. Michael E. Porter, *Competitive Strategy: Techniques for Analyzing Industries and Competitors* (New York, NY: The Free Press, 1980), p. 156.

15. Group Health Association of America, *Patterns in HMO Enrollment* (Washington, DC: Group Health Association of America, 1994), p. 7.

16. Ibid., pp. 7-8.

17. Interstudy Publications, *The Interstudy Competitive Edge, Volume 4, Number 1* (Minneapolis, MN: Interstudy Publications, 1994), p. 10.

18. David W. Emmon and Carol J. Simon, "Recent Trends in Managed Care" in *Socioeconomic Characteristics of Medical Practice 1994* (Chicago, IL: American Medical Association, 1994), pp. 25-33.

19. E.W. Hoy, Richard Curtis and Thomas Rice, "Change and Growth in Managed Care" in *Health Affairs* (Winter 1991), pp. 18-36.

20. Alliance for Healthcare Strategy and Marketing, "Employers Attempt to Cut Costs Without Reform" in *Managed Care Competitive Network*, Vol. 3, Issue 1 (1994), p. 1.

21. Ibid.

22. Sandra Christenson, "Effects on Managed Care: An Update," *Congressional Budget Office* (March 1994).

23. Jon Gabel, "The Health Insurance Picture in 1993: Some Rare Good News" in *Health Affairs* (13:327, Spring 1994).

24. Alliance for Healthcare Strategy and Marketing, "GTE's Creative Approach to Healthcare Coverage" in *The Alliance Bulletin* (November/December 1994).

25. Chris Coulter, Helen Darling, and Gary Goldstein, "Meeting the Needs of Large Employers" in *HMO Magazine* (January/February 1995), pp. 9-11.

26. HMO Managers Letter, "Study Finds HMO Members More Satisfied Than Those in FFS, Regardless of Health Status" (October 1994).

27. Ibid.

28. Christina Pope, "Nine of 10 Practices Have Managed Care Contracts" in *MGM Update* (March 1995), p. 11.

29. "Managed Care Market Forces Increase Demand for Some Health Care Professionals" in *Managed Care Competitive Network*, Vol. 3, Issue 1 (1994).

30. Ibid.

31. Joel Goldberg, "Doctor's Earnings Take a Nose-dive" in *Medical Economics* (September 12, 1994), pp. 123-132.

32. Jonathan P. Weiner, "Forecasting the Effects of Health Reform on US Physician Workforce Requirements" in *Journal of the American Medical Association*, Vol. 272, No. 3 (July 20,1994), pp. 222-230.

33. Rhonda J. Peebles, "Preferred Provider Organizations: A Review and Update" in *American College of Surgeons Bulletin* (77:33, September 1992).

34. "Competition, Incentives to Recruit Family Practitioners Escalates, Survey Report Says" in MGM Update (March 1995).

35. Interstudy Publications, *The Interstudy Competitive Edge,* Vol. 4, No. 1 (Minneapolis, MN: Interstudy Publications, 1994), p. 43.

36. Marianne Hurewitz, "Physician Partners" in *HMO Magazine* (January/February 1995), pp. 13-14.

37. Ibid.

38. Ibid.

39. Ibid.

40. Steven Findlay, "How New Alliances are Changing Health Care" in *Business and Health* (October 1993), p. 28.

41. Frank Cerne, "The Fading Stand Alone Hospital" in *Hospitals and Health Networks* (June 20,1994), p. 28.

42. *Group Practice Managed Healthcare News*, Vol. 10, No. 2 (February 1994), p. 10.

43. American Health Consultants, "New Report Offers Life and Death Perspective on Future of PHOs" in *PHO Update*, Vol. 2, No. 3 (March 1995), pp. 1-3.

44. American Medical Association, *Medical Groups in the US–A Survey of Practice Characteristics* (1993).

45. Christina Pope, "Nine of 10 Practices Have Managed Care Contracts" in *MGM Update* (March 1995), p. 11.

46. Ibid.

47. Managed Healthcare, "Defining the Future of Integrated Delivery" in *Managed Healthcare* (April 1995), p. 28.

48. Julie Johnson, "Integrated Networks are Expensive" in *AMA News,* 1994.

49. "Defining the Future of Integrated Delivery" in *Managed Healthcare* (April 1995), p. 22.

50. "The Fading Stand Alone Hospital."

51. Mark Hagland, "Merger Mania?" in *Hospitals and Health Networks* (May 20, 1994), p. 46.

52. Ibid.

53. Alliance for Healthcare Marketing and Strategy, "Columbia/HCA's Nationwide Integrated Delivery System" in *The Alliance Bulletin* (November/December 1994), pp. 3,6.

54. Ibid.

55. Sharon McEachern, "Missing Links" in *HMO Magazine* (November/December 1994), p. 51.

56. Robert Fromberg and Barry S. Bader, "Information Systems for Managed Care" in *Health System Leader*, Vol. 1, No. 8 (October 1994), pp. 4-14.

57. McEachern, "Missing Links," p. 51.

58. "Digital Video-On-Demand Net for Healthcare," *Newsbytes News Network* (April 6, 1995).

59. Ron Winslow, "Welfare Recipients are a Hot Commodity in Managed Care Now" in *The Wall Street Journal* (April 12, 1995), p. 1.

60. Health Care Financing Administration, *Fiscal Year 1996 Justification*, pp. 14, 26.

61. Diane Rowland, *Medicaid: A Program in Transition–The Federal-State Partnership for Health Care Reform: The Role of 1115 Demonstration Waivers*, (Washington, DC: The Kaiser Commission on the Future of Medicaid, March 1995), chart 19.

62. Lisa Nolan, Trish Riley, and Jane Horvath, *Less Federal Funding for Medicaid: Is State Flexibility the Answer?* (Portland, ME: National Academy for State Health Policy, April, 1995), p. 3.

63. Nolan, Lisa; Riley, Trish; and Horvath, Jane, *Less Federal Funding for Medicaid: Is State Flexibility the Answer?*. (Washington, DC: National Academy for State Health Policy, April 1995), p. 1.

64. The Kaiser Commission on the Future of Medicaid, *Medicaid and Managed Care: Lessons Learned from the Literature*. (Washington, DC: The Kaiser Commission on the Future of Medicaid, 1995), p. 4.

65. Ibid.

66. June Stollman, "Medicaid, a New Frontier For Managed Care . . . but it's a Very Tough Sell" in *MGM Journal* (March/April 1995), p. 38.

67. The Henry J. Kaiser Family Foundation, "Medicare and Managed Care," May 1995.

68. Ibid.

69. Jill Wechsler, "Can Managed Care Rescue Medicare?" in *Managed Healthcare* (April 1995), p. 16.

70. Peter Yedidia, "Managed Risk Contracting," in *MGM Journal* (March/April 1995), p. 46.

71. Ibid.

72. Ibid.

73. David Coleman, "Medicare Risk Contracts" in *Managed Healthcare*, Vol. 5, No. 10 (October 1995), p. 38.

74. "Managed Eldercare" in *The Wall Street Journal* (April 27, 1995).

75. United States General Accounting Office, "Medicaid Managed Care–Enrollment Growth Underscores Need to Revamp HMO Payment Methods," GAO/T-HEHS-95-207 (Washington, DC: GAO, 1995), p. 7.

76. Randall S. Brown et al., "Do Health Maintenance Organizations Work for Medicare?" in *Health Care Financing Review*, Vol. 15, No. 1 (1993), p. 14.

77. Health Care Financing Administration, "Medicare Managed Care Program Update–1995," (Washington, DC, HCFA, 1995), p. 3.

78. Ibid., p. 6.

79. Jill Wechsler, "A Cornerstone of Seniors' Reform" in *Managed Healthcare*, Vol. 5, No. 11 (November 1995), p. 22.

80. Ibid.

CHAPTER 2:
HEALTH CARE BATTLEFIELDS

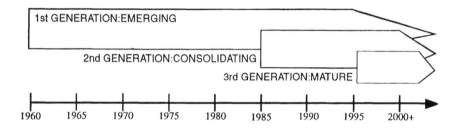

Of all of the trends and issues discussed in Chapter 1, market and cost pressures leading to the growth of managed care holds the most significance for the payer, medical delivery, and health care system marketer. However, the rate and degree of penetration of managed care varies greatly from local market to local market, and although it is possible to generically or universally define the health care marketer's role and responsibilities within the changing dynamic (see Chapter 6), trying to structure marketing objectives, strategies, and tactics on a generic or universal basis holds little if any value.

Market dynamics are closely related to managed care pressures in each local market. Payers, physicians, and hospitals must understand market dynamics in order to create market responsive organizations and to design marketing objectives, strategies, and tactics that will position and differentiate their organization for purposes of creating long-term, sustainable competitive advantage. For example, the dynamics of a fragmented market with low managed care penetration should drive the payers to focus strategic marketing activities upon differentiating and positioning against indemnity coverage via attributional level marketing (i.e., cost and benefit differences), while the dynamics of a highly penetrated, consolidated market with a few, large managed care competitors should drive the marketer to focus strategic marketing activities upon "mindset marketing" approaches such as brand differentiation to create an image and identity that speak to customer and prospect motivations to purchase.

As managed care penetration increases, market and organizational structures will evolve from fragmentation to consolidation of providers to federations of provider/payer organizations. Strategic marketing objectives will evolve from category growth, to product differentiation, to brand differentiation.

Within the health care industry there are three general types of battlefields. These market dynamics or structures each demand a different set of strategic and operational marketing initiatives and activities for payers, physicians, and hospitals. *Emerging markets* (referred to herein as the First Generation Battlefield) are characterized by low managed care penetration, a high degree of fragmentation, and arm's length relationships between payers and providers. *Consolidating markets* (referred to herein as the Second Generation Battlefield) have average managed care penetration rates, significant amounts of integration and consolidation activities between and among physicians, hospitals, and payers, and the creation of marketing functions and responsibilities within the medical delivery environment in addition to those performed by payers. *Mature markets* (referred to herein as the Third Generation Battlefield) have high managed care penetration and are characterized by competition among a small number of competitors who operate under a combined medical delivery/insurance umbrella.

While it is of critical importance for health care marketers to recognize dynamics within their markets, it is equally critical to recognize that markets evolve from one battlefield to another. What makes the marketer's task so complex is that there is no clear beginning or end to these generations, so the marketer must not only keep one foot in the present, responding or reacting to current market situations, but also must put one foot in the future such that he can position his organization to capitalize upon trends and changing dynamics proactively, rather than reactivity. Further, while categorization makes for easy analysis, in the real world markets will not fit neatly into the categories discussed below. In fact, it is quite possible that within any given market, characteristics of the three different types of markets may be present.

THE FIRST GENERATION BATTLEFIELD

According to the Marion Merrell Dow *Managed Care Digest Update* (1994) twelve states have managed care penetration rates of less than 5 percent, and four states–West Virginia, Vermont, Alaska, and Wyoming–have no HMO enrollment whatsoever. In fact, there are some fifteen states, according to *Update,* where managed care penetration is less than 10 percent.

On a First Generation Battlefield, managed care penetration is less than 10 percent, and providers are generally fragmented, that is, not organized into systems or networks to accept risk. Players in the market may include solo practitioners, group practices (single and multi-specialty), community and tertiary hospitals, IPA, and different types of payers including indemnity insurers (most prevalent), self-insured employers, and HMOs. There are few, if any, economies of scale in the market as a result of a lack of integration, and generally, contractual relationships between buyers and insurers are short in duration. Figure 2.1 presents a graphic representation of the First Generation Battlefield.

As managed care is a relatively new phenomena in the market, entry barriers for managed care organizations are low in terms of numbers of competitors and the ability to position against indemnity insurers, but high in terms of organizing medical delivery participants as initially, providers wish to maintain the status quo in terms of fee-based reimbursement. However, as managed care penetration grows, physicians and hospitals, for purposes of protecting market share, will seek a relationship with just about any payer dangling a contract.

FIGURE 2.1. The First Generation Battlefield

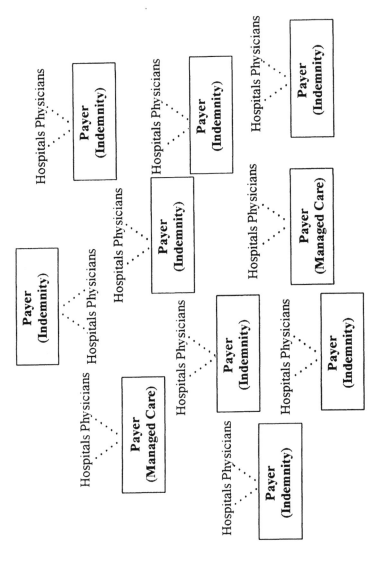

THE SECOND GENERATION BATTLEFIELD

The Rochester, New York health care market has consistently been used by industry experts as a model of cost containment. Built upon cooperation between hospitals, community rating practices, and a high managed care penetration rate, the system has produced health insurance premiums that are one-third less than the national average. The market shares of the two key insurers in the market, each of which offers an IPA HMO product, have not fluctuated substantially in the last five years, and consumers are unwavering in the levels of satisfaction they profess for both their insurance and medical delivery services.

Sounds ideal? Not quite. . . .

The health care industry in Rochester is experiencing unprecedented turmoil. What has been touted as managed care in the market is really nothing more than a pre-paid health plan based upon a discounted fee for service plus withhold negotiated with each and every physician practice separately. HMO products in the market are virtually indistinguishable in terms of benefits, premiums, out of pocket costs, and composition of the medical delivery system. Historically, product innovations brought to market by the smaller payer are quickly duplicated to negate competitive advantage, leaving the strong brand identity of the larger payer as the single key point of differentiation between the two companies.

Since hospital reimbursement in New York State is based upon DRGs (Diagnostic Related Groups) leaving little if any room for negotiations, Rochester's miracle has in fact been built upon the backs of physicians in the community. Consider, for example, that because there are only two payers of any consequence in the market controlling nearly 700,000 enrollees, physicians have very little latitude except to accept what the payers are willing to pay. While employers, employees and their dependents, and the payers are reaping the benefits the payer's market clout, physicians are becoming increasingly frustrated and motivated to act.

According to Lisa Brubaker, Executive Director of the Monroe County Medical Society, "physician compensation in the market is less than the national average. A pediatrician in Rochester, for example, merely has to travel the 70 miles or so to Buffalo to realize an increase in income" (Personal communication).

Effectively, physicians must belong to both IPAs in order to survive*, creating physician panels that are 1,800 to 2,000 physicians strong. While this might suggest that the IPAs wield considerable clout, the opposite is true. The IPAs serve mostly as a reimbursement conduit. Although angry at their situation, physicians in the market are fragmented and have historically been unable to organize a concerted effort to improve their lot, particularly in terms of organizing to accept and manage risk, and since the physicians' risk is spread over such a large base, the effect of utilization management is virtually negligible, as corrective action or sanctions against any given physician for excessive utilization have little effect upon the IPA as a whole.

Hospitals enjoy this status quo because if physicians create small, feisty organizations to accept and manage risk, they will witness a decrease in revenues as services are moved to an outpatient basis. The payers enjoy this status quo because fragmentation protects their market share by dissuading other payers from entering the market. The dynamic, however, is changing and the instrument of change is risk and reward.

Physicians have recognized that the way to increase their income and share of voice in the market is to take it away from the hospitals, and that the way to do so is to organize into small, market-responsive groups; accept risk (in the form of capitated payments from payers); and manage the delivery and utilization of medical services. Hospitals have recognized this threat, and to keep the physician market fragmented and the income stream within their own domain, they are buying physician practices and funding the development of risk-bearing Physician/Hospital Organizations (PHOs).

Payers have recognized that an organized, risk-bearing delivery system (whether sponsored by physicians or hospitals) lowers the entry barrier for other payers to enter Rochester, and they are taking a wait-and-see attitude before taking a conciliatory tack or deciding to flex their market clout in a yet-to-be-named manner. Concurrently, payers are seeking ways to foster sustainable and leverageable product differentiation—achievable through (for example) new products created from differently composited medical

---

*In New York State an IPA can only serve one HMO.

delivery systems. It is not unfeasible that future products in the market will be branded around identification of participating doctors and hospitals.

What a delightful mess!

This type of story is unfolding in markets across the country as the health care industry continues to evolve. Factors contributing to this evolutionary process are explored in this part of the book, as the health care system marketer of the future must recognize, understand, and react to the changing dynamic.

Characteristics of the Second Generation Battlefield include reducing health care costs as a means to reduce premium costs and/or improve margin; creating economies of scale to create cost and competitive advantages; decentralizing risk and accountability; and the initiation of efforts to squeeze excess capacity and overutilization out of the system. Perhaps the most significant characteristic of the Second Generation Battlefield is the structuring and design of organizations engineered to protect capital by minimizing or reducing expenditures. Cost-containment efforts–in particular, risk-based payment systems–spurred by rising health care costs are fostering economic concentration, consolidation, and vertical integration leading to the development of alliances, networks, consortiums, and other entities formed as a defense against an increasingly hostile environment[1] where market share, access to capital, and access to management expertise will separate winners from losers.

Generally, managed care penetration on the Second Generation Battlefield will range between 10 and 30 percent. In order to maximize marketability, payers will resort to product mix expansion, where numerous types of managed care products are developed and launched, ranging from limited access plans centered around group or staff model HMOs to open access plans, such as Point-of-Service, (POS) mixing managed care and indemnity elements. The ultimate effect is a confusing mix and number of managed care products with different cost and benefit characteristics, targeted to the 70 to 90 percent of the market not in a managed care product.

The structure of the battlefield is also characterized by changes in the relationship between payers and providers as providers assume more financial risk and as payers move toward focusing on administrative and marketing activities. Consolidations of the medical delivery system begin to occur as physicians increasingly organize into groups (single and multispecialty), and as hospitals merge or sell to large national concerns creating economies of scale.

On the Second Generation Battlefield, the importance and clout of Primary Care Physicians grows dramatically, while hospitals and specialists face decreasing revenues and income as excess capacity becomes a strategic target of integrated delivery system organizers. The market is cluttered with chaos and strategic uncertainty where mergers, acquisitions, alliances, and more are born out of fear and confusion. Hospitals, in particular, seek to capture and bind PCPs to the institution through mechanisms ranging from practice acquisitions to creation of Management Services Organizations (MSOs) and Physician/Hospital Organizations (PHOs). A key outcome of this chaos is fragmented accountability for quality, outcomes, utilization, cost control, and customer satisfaction.

While there are many facets to the Second Generation Battlefield, understanding local market dynamics represents the key to growth–or survival–for combatants. We are, in effect, now witnessing the creation of new types of structural and contractual relationships that are driving new sets of strategic objectives.

In the Second Generation environment, under certain circumstances or situations, any player or combination of players can exert financial and political pressures over other players to produce long-term, strategically based competitive advantages. Assuming that the flow of health care dollars in a market is fixed, money and patients and ultimately power within a market shifts with the application of pressure which can take forms ranging from risk-sharing arrangements to strategic alliances to mergers and acquisitions. For example, in a market where hospital occupancy is low, a payer can pressure hospitals to obtain a better deal by trading their market share for a guarantee of occupancy at a discounted rate. Or, in a market where managed care penetration is high and physicians–particularly PCPs–are organized, their ability to secure favorable capitation arrangements and capture utilization savings through exercise of their gatekeeper responsibilities is significant.

Figure 2.2 provides a graphic representation of a Second Generation Battlefield.

FIGURE 2.2. The Second Generation Battlefield

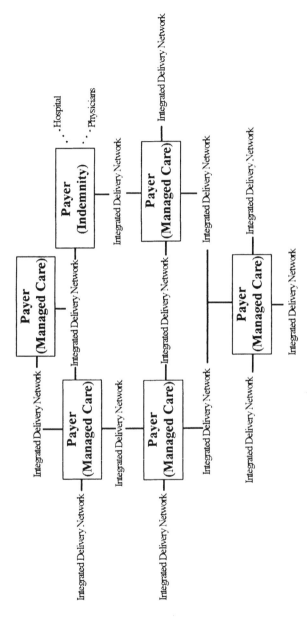

THE THIRD GENERATION BATTLEFIELD

The Third Generation Battlefield is the most highly penetrated market from a managed care perspective, with penetration rates ranging to over 30 percent. It is, therefore, a market where managed care is well established, and consequently, a market where category growth strategies give way to market share battles based upon differentiation between managed care organizations. On the Third Generation Battlefield, excess capacity and overutilization will be significantly reduced and most, if not all medical risk will be directly in the hands of providers. Patients in this environment will contribute to these reductions, as an increasing burden will be placed upon them to be accountable for their health and use of medical delivery resources.

There are relatively few, and indeed it might be argued that there are no, Third Generation Battlefields in existence today. It represents, however, a logical expansion of the war in the health care industry from the perspective that the drive for competitive advantage must inevitably result in maximization of cost reductions from both clinical and administrative perspectives. Achieving this goal will be a function of further consolidations, efforts aimed at eliminating excess capacity and overutilization, the development of exclusive payer/medical delivery relationships, and the structuring of large organizations to foster economies of scale.

Consequently, one of the most significant characteristics of this type of market will be a reduction in the number of competitive health care systems, as those health care plans who can deliver economies of scale in terms of administrative and marketing costs will secure a competitive advantage and drive smaller, weaker players out of the market or into a merger or acquisition. Medical delivery and insurance/administrative functions will co-reside within these large organizations, yet, all participants regardless of whether they are employees or exclusive contractors, will share accountability for clinical and financial results as cost and performance incentives come into alignment.

Customers on the Third Generation Battlefield will thus have fewer choices relative to selection of a health care system, and battles for market share will not so much be a function of product differentiation as brand differentiation. However, these customers will be knowledgeable, demanding, and sophisticated, basing their selection around a combination of brand affinity and information on quality, costs, and outcomes. In this market, both customers and the health care system will seek long term, multiyear contracts. Figure 2.3 presents a graphic depiction of the Third Generation Battlefield.

Finally, as the market shrinks in terms of systems but continues growing from a managed care penetration perspective, the concept of *community health outcomes* will be of critical importance. In addition to responsibility for the health and financial concerns of customers, health care systems will also be responsible for contributing to improving the overall status of the health of people living in the market.

Combatants in the Third Generation Battlefield will build health information systems that can identify patterns of clinical practice and patient behavior for specific diseases or patient populations. These systems, according to John Eichert of the Hastings Health Care Group, will create the ability to focus on disease prevention and health promotion strategies that reduce demand. Taken on a community-wide basis, it is not unreasonable to postulate that community-wide health improvement efforts, driven by coalitions of government and the large health care systems in the market, will be undertaken.

STRATEGIC MARKETING IMPLICATIONS

Market dynamics and structures define the health care battlefield. In turn, characteristics of the battlefield will define appropriate strategic marketing initiatives for payers, physicians, and hospitals. Ultimately, these initiatives have critical marketing implications that must be acted upon in order to ensure survival, at worst, and prosperity, at best.

Consequently, every type of participant in the health care industry—payer, physician, and hospital—must face and address three critical questions:

1. Is our market a First, Second, or Third Generation Battlefield?
2. Based upon this assessment, what do we do to survive or prosper right now?
3. What should we do to position ourselves for the next evolutionary step?

FIGURE 2.3. The Third Generation Battlefield

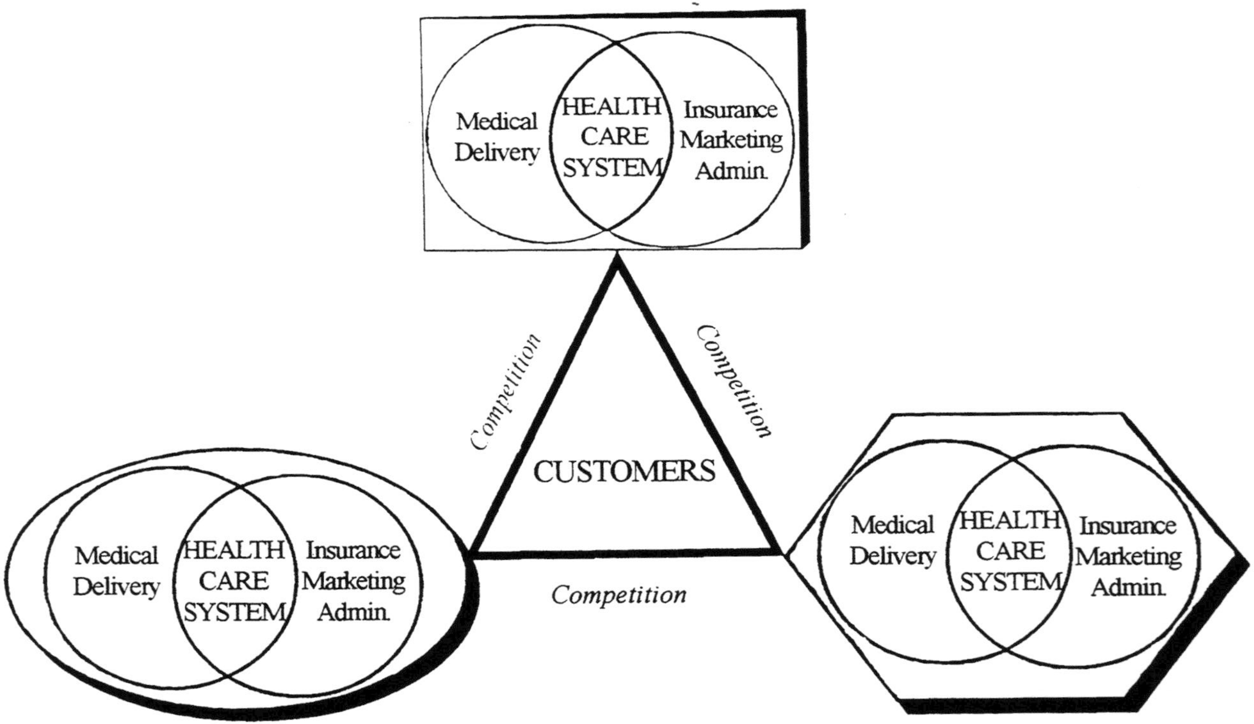

Is Our Market a First, Second, or Third Generation Battlefield?

In order to develop strategic and tactical plans for capitalizing upon market dynamics and structures, payers, providers, and physicians must first understand the playing field, for the type of market in which they operate will drive both current and future strategic initiatives. Understanding the market involves analysis of factors ranging from managed care penetration to health care plan choices for customers. Table 2.1 provides a tool which can be helpful in conducting this analysis.

As might be inferred from this table, the likelihood of any one market falling exactly within all of the defined parameters is low. It is more likely that a market will show a mix of characteristics; for example, moderate managed care penetration but few health care systems present; or the dominance of exclusive relationships in a market where national medical management or hospital chains are not present, and so on.

For purposes of analysis and, ultimately, the ability to define and execute strategic and tactical actions against the type of market, three types of criteria are most critical: managed care penetration; relationships between and among physicians, hospitals and payers; and risk relationships. These are identified in Table 2.1 as "Critical Factors." As markets evolve, the higher the managed care penetration the closer the relationships between and among payers and providers will be, and the greater the likelihood that financial incentives between payers and providers will be aligned.

What Must We Do to Survive or Prosper Right Now?

Once the type of market has been defined, participants must next turn to defining the strategic and tactical activities that are most appropriate to ensuring their survival or prosperity. These will differ from type of market to type of market, as financial incentives shift with the degree of penetration of managed care.

For example, on the First Generation Battlefield, both hospitals and physicians will seek to maintain the status quo in terms of reimbursement (generally FFS) and clinical autonomy. Since managed care payers need a medical delivery panel in order to deliver a product, the provider's ability to negotiate a status quo will be

TABLE 2.1. Market Assessment Tool

CRITICAL FACTORS	1st Generation	2nd Generation	3rd Generation
Managed care penetration	Low	Moderate	High
Extent of physician consolidations into risk bearing entities	Limited	Feverish	Consolidations accomplished
Extent of hospital mergers, consolidations, alliance	Limited	Feverish	Consolidations accomplished
Extent of physician acquisition activities by hospitals	Limited	Feverish	Consolidations accomplished
Extent, presence of integrated delivery networks	Limited	Present	Dominant
Extent of risk bearing by medical delivery participants	Limited	Significant capitation activity	Global capitation
Extent of exclusive payer/provider relationships	Limited	Present	Dominant
SECONDARY FACTORS			
Presence of national medical management organizations	Limited	Present	Dominant
Presence of national hospital chains	Limited	Present	Very likely
Need for sophisticated MIS	Small	Necessary	Critical
Length of relationships between health care system and buyers	Short term	Short to mid-term	Long term
Concerted actions relative to community health outcomes, programs, and activities	Small	Growing	Critical
Health care plan choices for customers	Moderate	Many	Moderate
Health care systems present in market	Few to many	Saturated	Few

relatively high. On the other hand, payers will introduce some forms of utilization control, for example, a gatekeeper concept and some types of case management, representing the first steps in squeezing excess utilization and capacity out of the market.

From the health care system perspective, the key marketing responsibility on the First Generation Battlefield lies in the payer's domain, with the critical goal of moving employers and employees into managed care. They must create awareness of both the category and their plan, capitalizing upon cost and benefit differences, while minimizing negative perceptions related to access issues. Questions faced by the health care marketer include:

1. How do we grow the category of managed care?
2. How do we create preference for our insurance plan?
3. Does it make sense for us to partner?
4. What evidence exists to suggest that managed care penetration will increase?
5. What should I be doing to prepare for increased managed care penetration?

A key responsibility of payers, physicians, and hospitals on the Second Generation Battlefield is careful, considered, strategic analysis to capitalize upon the changing dynamic of the health care industry. Whether the objective is to secure a sustainable competitive advantage, or maintain the status quo, or even survive, the ability to "read" the environment is of paramount importance to developing appropriate strategic initiatives. Among key environmental considerations for the marketer to note are:

–hospital occupancy	–physician fragmentation
–market share/dominance of key payers	–share/dominance of key hospitals
–brand identification, perception	–PCP strengths
–competitive strengths, weaknesses	–regulatory based opportunities
–managed care penetration	(i.e. Medicaid)
–self-funding employers	–managed care legislation
–employer cost reduction pressures	

On the Second Generation Battlefield, payers will seek to grow market share and profits via category growth and product differentiation marketing activities. They may attempt to capitalize upon provider fragmentation by direct contracting while concurrently using their size as a tool for negotiating favorable, risk-based contracts. Hospitals face significant cost pressures on the Second Generation Battlefield, as payers and physician-based networks seek to squeeze excess capacity out of the market. Their key strategic objectives may center around a combination of mergers, primary care acquisitions, and willingness to accept capitated reimbursement in order to maximize their control over the flow of health care dollars and to capture as much of the market's medical delivery system as feasibly possible.

Physicians on the Second Generation Battlefield have the opportunity to make the biggest gains relative to capturing health care dollars, market share, and clinical control via the development of risk-taking physician's networks. Primary care networks, in particular, stand to gain the most. In discussions with PCPs across the country, the following reasons for forming a primary care network are commonly cited:

- Increased market leverage in a managed care environment
- Greater negotiating power for physicians and hospitals
- More economic efficiencies, including standardized clinical procedures and administration
- Expanded geographic reach and growth for group practices
- Improved professional lifestyle
- Acceptance and management of capitation
- Securing capital to support recruiting efforts[2]

Table 2.2 describes strategic objectives, implications of those objectives, and a number of initiatives and options for consideration by payers, hospitals, and physicians. This table describes the Second Generation Battlefield as an environment where conflicting interests, driven by new financial dynamics and self-preservation concerns, drive strategic opportunities. Within this chaotic landscape, health care marketers need to assume responsibility for creating and delivering products to capitalize upon their institution's strengths and opportunities while redressing weaknesses and threats.

On the Third Generation Battlefield, the battle is concluded as the market is dominated by large health care systems characterized by exclusive relationships between payers and a medical delivery system or network. These relationships may take forms ranging from employment to exclusive contracts between an integrated delivery network and a payer organization.

Now, the marketing function is basically external in nature; that is, the health care system assumes responsibility for acquiring covered lives. The key difference in the shift from payer only to health care system marketing lies in the fact that everybody in the system must hold marketing accountability. As markets evolve, it is inevitable and necessary for the health care system to move from product-driven to market-driven strategies. In other words, the marketing focus shifts from delivering products to delivering services corresponding to the market's needs. This shift in the Third Generation poses a demand for *every participant* regardless of whether they are the CEO of a hospital or the receptionist at a physician's office or the head of the health care system's Marketing Department, to become involved in marketing and sales functions. Dr. William Flexner, for example, maintains that:

> To create a truly market-driven organization, the marketing function must be involved not only in the development of external strategies (e.g., packaging, price, distribution and promotion), but also be expanded to include the creation of an internal culture that makes the design and delivery of service responsive to customers served. Creation of a market-driven organization (that is, the diffusion throughout the organization of the single message that "meeting customer expectations is what we are all about") is significantly different than creation of a marketing department within an organization. If an organization is going to truly become market-driven, its management must integrate critical aspects of the marketing function in the jobs and compensation of managers and employees throughout the organization.[3]

Consequently, financial incentives in the Third Generation Battlefield may expand beyond enrollment and utilization goals to include retention and customer satisfaction goals. The creation and execution of programs to these ends will become an integral part of the marketer's responsibility, and activities designed to increase the awareness and change the behaviors of "employees" toward an obsession with customer needs and satisfaction will become one of the most challenging aspects of their job.

What Should We Do to Position Ourselves for the Next Evolutionary Step?

Beyond just meeting current strategic needs, payers, physicians, and hospitals must concurrently keep an eye to the future in order to

TABLE 2.2. The Second Generation Battlefield

	Strategic Objectives	Risk/Reimbursement Implications
Payer	• Retention, growth of market share • Profitability • Cost control via risk management and administrative efficiencies and use of size as tool for negotiating clout with providers • Capitalize upon provider fragmentation (especially MD) where possible; buy providers where appropriate; create provider alliances where necessary	• Attempt to pass risk to providers via mechanisms ranging from withholds to global capitation • Give bonus or sanctions depending upon utilization patterns, patient satisfaction • Address pressure from hospitals, MDs, networks–dependent upon degree of cohesiveness–to maintain status quo
Hospital	• Retention, growth of market share • Profitability • Maximize utilization of facility • Stem erosion IP/OP "transfers" • Survival • If capitated, capture utilization $ • Create strong brand identity and consumer loyalty as barrier to payer clout • Capitalize upon MD fear, insecurity, and gain loyalty via PHOs, MSOs	• Address pressures from payers to share risk (per diem, case rates, partial capitation, full capitation) • Subject to pressures from MD networks and payers to deliver high quality at lowest possible cost • Look for opportunities to pass risk down to physicians • Capture utilization savings
Physician	• Survival, retention of market share • Maintain clinical autonomy • PCPs: leverage clout through creation of large PCP networks • Specialists: capture market share via securing exclusive contracts • Via networks & IPAs, where possible, use size as negotiating clout to strike favorable deals with payers and hospitals	• Increasing movement away from FFS to capitation • Opportunity to increase income via utilization savings, particularly from institution • Subject to pressures from payers, hospitals, payer/hospital alliances to assume increasing levels of risk while producing high quality outcomes at lowest possible cost

	Clinical Implications	**Strategic Initiatives and Opportunities**
Payer	• Payer as "regulator" of utilization • Payer's Medical Director wielding increasing amount of power	• Creation of limited delivery networks to create new products • HMO consolidations to gain • share, size, and negotiating clout • Use of mortality/outcome data to enforce utilization protocols • Payer/MD bonding programs, like MSOs, to secure physician loyalty • Acquisition of PCP practices to limit PCP network formation
Hospital	• Subject to treatment guidelines and protocols, outcomes, and measures • Increasing importance of patient encountering data • Low-cost and risk-sharing pressures create cost/quality tensions; pressures to reduce IP days • Increasing importance of patient satisfaction	• Shift to ambulatory care to capture outpatient leakage • Hospital mergers and creation of hospital networks for share and size • Hospital/MD bonding programs like PHOs, to secure physician loyalty • Acceptance of capitation to retain utilization savings • Acquisition of PCP practices to limit PCP network formation and to maximize utilization savings
Physician	• Subject to treatment guidelines and protocols, outcomes, and measures • Increasing importance of encountering data • Low-cost and risk-sharing pressures create cost/quality tensions • Increasing importance of patient satisfaction	• Group practice development for economic and security purposes • Formation of alliances, networks to leverage clout • Acceptance of capitation to retain utilization savings • Strategic alliances with payers to protect share

survive and prosper. If evolution from one type of market to another is indeed inevitable, it makes sense to devote strategic planning thinking and resources to position the organization to capitalize upon, rather than to merely react, to change and chaos.

Regardless of stage of evolution or transition, and regardless of payer, physician, or hospital, a critical marketing responsibility is a continuing analysis and assessment of market situation and environment. Having an understanding of activities in the market, from managed care enrollment growth to the types and extent of medical delivery system consolidations and alliances, is crucial to positioning the organization for transition.

As the market evolves from a first to second generation status, payers should be seeking to move people into managed care through the creation and launch of multiple managed care products. Concurrently, they should be instituting increasingly stricter medical utilization controls and passing an increasing amount of risk to providers in order to realign financial incentives. Physicians, in order to maintain autonomy and clinical, financial, and administrative control must begin the process of organizing into risk-bearing entities, while seeking opportunities to join or create integrated delivery networks. Hospitals too should be looking for integrated delivery network opportunities, while evaluating opportunities to merge, sell, or create hospital alliances or networks. Additionally, hospitals might consider primary care practice acquisition, as control over the medical delivery system and the ability to retain health care dollars that can be realized through this strategy is the foundation for participation on the Second Generation Battlefield.

As markets evolve to Third Generation status, both hospitals and physicians must be willing and able to operate within a managed care environment from cost and clinical management perspectives. Both hospitals and physicians should be considering and evaluating opportunities for forming an exclusive relationship with a payer, as alignments into large health care systems will be necessary for survival. Payers too should be seeking and evaluating exclusive relationships, as well as evaluating merger or consolidation opportunities.

Table 2.3 provides an overview of positioning activities for market transitions. Table 2.4 provides a summary overview of the characteristics of the three generations of health care battlefields.

TABLE 2.3. Positioning for the Next Evolutionary Step

	<u>1st to 2nd Generation Evolution</u>	<u>2nd to 3rd Generation Evolution</u>
Physician	1) Continue taking the pulse of the market in terms of: • managed care penetration • hospital initiatives to acquire practices • hospital initiatives to create PHOs • market entry by national medical management companies • market entry by national hospital chains 2) Defragmentation: organize to risk bearing entities 3) Seek/evaluate opportunities to create or join an integrated delivery network 4) Acquire, use sophisticated MIS 5) Seek/evaluate managed care contracting opportunities	1) Continue taking the pulse of the market in terms of: • managed care penetration • payer mergers, acquisitions, alliances • hospital mergers, acquisitions, alliances • trends toward development of exclusive relationships 2) Adapt to operating within a managed care environment from cost and clinical management perspectives 3) Evaluate advantages, disadvantages of opportunities for exclusive relationships
Hospital	1) Continue taking the pulse of the market in terms of: • managed care penetration • development of risk-bearing physician organizations • market entry by national medical management companies • market entry by national hospital chains 2) Seek/evaluate opportunities to acquire PCPs 3) Seek/evaluate opportunities to create or join an integrated delivery network 4) Seek/evaluate opportunites to create hospital based alliances, networks, etc. 5) Evaluate opportunities to merge or sell 6) Acquire/use sophisticated MIS 7) Seek/evaluate managed care contracting opportunities	Same as above

TABLE 2.3 (continued)

<u>1st to 2nd Generation Evolution</u>	<u>2nd to 3rd Generation Evolution</u>
Payer 1) Continue taking the pulse of the market in terms of: • managed care penetration • customer attitudes toward managed care • medical delivery consolidations, mergers, network development activities 2) Create, launch multiple managed care products 3) Seek opportunities to pass risk down to medical delivery system 4) Convert indemnity covered lives to managed care covered lives 5) Seek control over medical utilization 6) Create differentiation through products, product mix	1) Seek/evaluate opportunities for developing exclusive relationships with medical delivery systems, IDNs 2) Seek/evaluate opportunities to merge, consolidate, sell to other payers 3) Seek long-term relationships with buyers 4) Seek involvement in community health care outcome efforts 5) Establish a branded identity

TABLE 2.4. Characteristics of the Three Generations of Health Care Battlefields

	1st Generation: Emerging Health Care Systems	2nd Generation: Consolidating Health Care Systems	3rd Generation: Mature Health Care Systems
Managed Care Penetration	Less than 10 percent	10 to 30 percent	Over 30 percent
Market Structure	• Fragmented: providers are not organized into systems or networks to accept risk, payers generally contract individually with providers or through provider groups • Contractual, arm's length relationships between payers and providers • Little if any economies of scale as a result of lack of integration • Short-term relationships between buyers and insurers	• Consolidating; providers organizing into alliances, partnerships, joint ventures, networks, etc. and then contracting with payers on a risk/capitated basis • Rise of integrated delivery systems/networks • High cost of integration forces participants to seek capital • Relationship between payers and providers begins to change as providers assume more financial risk and as payers move toward focusing upon administration and marketing activities • Economies of scale grow as hospitals merge or sell to large national concerns • Mega-HMO consolidations • Physicians increasingly organize into groups: single and multi-specialty • Health care system—the combination of medical delivery and insurance—begins to emerge and gain strength as a marketing concept	• Limited number of large health care systems competing for subscribers: combined insurance and integrated medical delivery under one organizational entity • Financial incentives of providers and payers aligned • Solo physician practices and solo hospitals become non-competitive • Economies of scale maximized • Long-term relationships established between buyers and the health care system • Sophisticated buyers: knowledgeable and demanding

83

TABLE 2.4 (continued)

Market Dynamics	• Managed care as a relatively new phenomena • Providers seek to maintain status quo in terms of fee-based reimbursement • Low overall entry barriers for managed care, particularly in terms of positioning against indemnity plans • HMOs lack clout in terms of size to secure advantages in dealing with buyers and suppliers • Physician incentives represented by intervention and volume • Hospital incentives represented by high occupancy, high charges, and high utilization	• Increasing importance and clout of PCPs • Physicians seek to protect market share and clinical autonomy from financial managers • Hospitals and specialists face decrease in revenues and income as PCP clout grows and as utilization and excess capacity become targets of cost cutters • Risk assumption on part of providers changes nature of relationship with payers • Chaos and strategic uncertainty; mergers, acquisitions, alliances, partnerships born out of fear and confusion • Local market as a battlefield: structures being created to capitalize upon fragmentation and weaknesses in market, hospitals in particular seek to capture and bind PCPs to institution • Confusing number of different managed care products with different cost, and benefit characteristics • Fragmented accountability for quality, utilization, cost, and customer satisfaction	• Managed care dominates the market • Excess capacity and overutilization virtually eliminated • Increasing burden on patient to be accountable for their health care and use of health care system • System-wide accountability for results in terms of quality, outcomes, utilization, cost, and customer satisfaction • Health care system positioned as a brand, brand differentiation achieved through composition and quality indices of medical delivery system • Product differentiation on basis of benefits and costs becomes difficult to achieve as a function of rapidity of competitive reactions; new products and applications difficult to develop and launch • Fewer choices for customers • Information systems (and use of data) becomes the life force of the health care system
Organizational Structures	Solo practitioners Group practice (single and multi-specialty) Community and tertiary hospitals Independent practice associations HMOs Indemnity insures Self-employed insures	**Existing** Solo practitioners Group practice Community, tertiary hospital IPAs HMOs Indemnity insurers Self-employed insurers **New** Physician networks Hospital networks PHOs MSOs Provider/payer alliances	Health care system: integrated medical delivery and insurance, administrative, and marketing functions under one organizational umbrella

REFERENCE NOTES

1. Myron D. Fottler and Donna Malvey, "Multiprovider Systems" in *Health Care Administration–Principles, Practices, Structure, and Delivery*, ed. Lawrence F. Wolper (Gaithersburg, MD: Aspen Publishers, Inc., 1995), pp. 489-515.

2. KPMG Peat Marwick, "Taking Action: Developing a Successful Primary Care Network" in *Health Care Reform–Building the Next Generation of Health Delivery Systems* (April 1994).

3. William A. Flexner, "Creating the Market Driven Organization: Focus on the Manufacture of Service is Key" in *Marketing is Everybody's Business*, ed. Peter Sanchez (Chicago, IL: Academy for Health Services Marketing, 1988), pp. 31-34.

CHAPTER 3:
HEALTH CARE PLAN STRUCTURES AND SYSTEMS

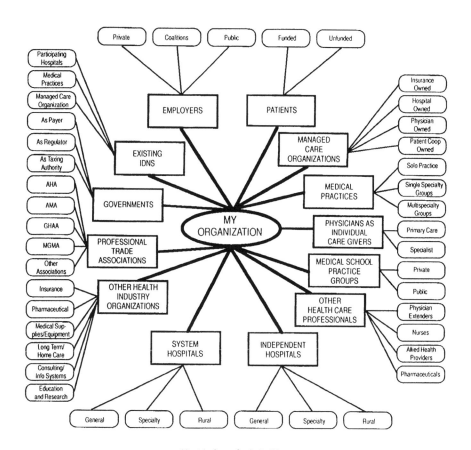

Health Care Stakeholders

From the modified Delphi study called "Facing the Uncertain Future," by the Medical Group Management Association and Texas Tech University (funding provided by Abbott Laboratories). Reprinted from: Blair, John D., Myron D. Fottler, Andrea Paolino, Timothy M. Rotarius, *Medical Group Practices Face the Uncertain Future: Challenges, Opportunities, and Strategies.* Englewood, CO: Center for Research in Ambulatory Health Care Administration (CRAHCA), 1995.

In a study conducted by the Medical Group Management Association and Texas Tech University titled "Facing the Uncertain Future," health care experts were asked to comment on the status of the health care industry in 1994 when the study began and their predictions for change by 1999. Major findings include:

1. The continued movement of the U.S. health industry from a primarily private insurance industry to one in which medical groups and hospitals will be members of integrated delivery systems/networks;
2. The increasing dominance of the components of integrated delivery systems/networks in 1999 (components are defined as medical practices, system hospitals, managed care organizations, and IDNs);
3. The potential effects of IDNs on the health care industry including increases in cost effectiveness, quality of administrative management, and the quality of physician leadership, as well as decreases in the availability of advanced medical technology and the duplication of ancillary services, facilities, and equipment.[1]

The authors also postulate that "key stakeholders in the health care arena are changing. . . . (They) include any individuals, groups or organizations who have clout or a stake in the decisions and actions of an organization and who attempt to influence those decisions and actions."[2] As shown in the diagram at the beginning of this chapter, stakeholders of the organization include employers, existing IDNs, government, professional trade associations, other health industry organizations, system hospitals, independent hospitals, patients, managed care organizations, medical practices, physicians as individual care givers, medical school practice groups, and other health care professionals. Identification of an organization's stakeholders is particularly crucial to strategic planning and analysis.

From another perspective, the health care organization's stakeholders might also be viewed, in toto, as a health care system. In other words, all of the elements described above must have some type of working relationship in order to deliver an insured health care product. The nature of these relationships, particularly in legal terms, and the degree of uniformity and congruity of vision and mission among the system's components will define the type of health care system. In turn, each type of health care system will have different strategic marketing needs, issues, objectives, and target markets. There are three types of health care systems. *Autonomous* health care systems center around contractual relationships between the payer and some number of independent and unrelated physicians, physician groups, and hospitals. IPA HMOs models are most representative of this type of system, and many indemnity plan/provider relationships can also be characterized under this system. *Synergistic* health care systems are formed through a contractual relationship between an integrated delivery network and a payer. Network model HMOs are an example of a synergistic system. In the *homogenous* health care system, payers and providers operate under one organizational entity, where providers exclusively perform for the entity. Both Group and Staff model HMOs can be considered as homogenous systems.

In relation to the types of health care battlefields (emerging, consolidating, mature), any type of health care system can be found in any type of battlefield. From a strategic marketing perspective, however, it is critical to understand that within any given local market, these systems may be in competition against one another for accounts, enrollees, and, in some cases, medical delivery participants. Selection of what type of plan to create or join, therefore, becomes of paramount importance for the payer, physician, and hospital.

The decision to join or create depends to a very large degree upon the market's maturity for managed care: the more mature the market, the greater the need will be to join or create an entity that can seize or maintain a competitive advantage in the changing dynamic. As managed care cost pressures increase in a market, the need for aligning financial incentives grows. As financial incentives grow, the relationship between provider and payer must be stronger. The stronger the relationship, the better able the opportunity to control premium and utilization, and expense costs in a mutually agreeable manner.

As relationships strengthen, the tendency to move from autonomous to synergistic to homogenous relationships grows. This is not to suggest that a linear or one-to-one relationship exists between type of battlefield and most appropriate health care plan/structure.

Rather, it suggests that as managed care penetration and cost control pressures increase within a market, those systems with the strongest payer/provider relationships *should be best positioned* to create and sustain a competitive advantage because their financial and clinical incentives should be aligned in a manner to produce a high quality, low cost product.

While in theory this makes sense, reality does not always correspond. For example, regardless of managed care penetration, consumer preference for an open panel may be the single most important factor driving market preference for an autonomous system. Or, the management controls within a homogenous system may be so poor that their medical costs are higher than competitive plans in the market, and consequently, higher premiums are required. What this suggests is that a combination of theory and market realities should drive a payer or provider to decide between join or create, where a careful assessment of market situation, competitors, and customer preference ultimately suggest the most appropriate and competitively advantageous health care system or structure for the battlefield.

Based upon the premise that the health care system is a product, it is apparent that depending upon type of system, the product will change from insurance to insurance plus medical delivery to an insurance/medical delivery entity. And the responsibility for marketing the health care system will change, as shown in Figure 3.1, from payer to payer and medical delivery system marketer to a health care system marketer.

FIGURE 3.1. Evolution of Marketing Responsibility

THE AUTONOMOUS HEALTH CARE SYSTEM

A distinct feature of autonomous health care systems is the arm's length relationship between payers and providers as shown in Figure 3.2. In an autonomous health care system, contractual relation-

FIGURE 3.2. The Autonomous Health Care System

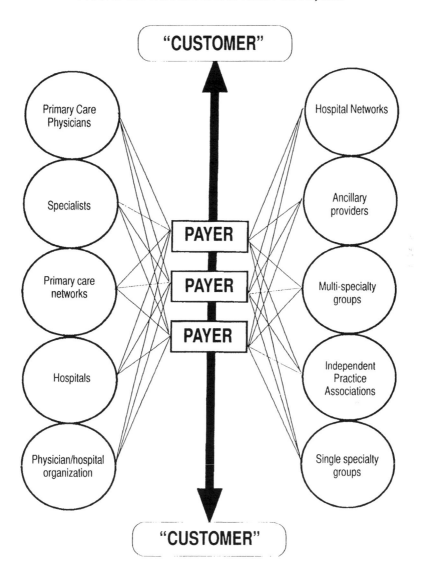

ships are established between individual providers (or through associations of providers like an Independent Practice Association) on a nonexclusive basis, and providers will generally contract with more than one payer in order to protect market share. Consequently, financial incentives for acting as a unified whole between and among participants in this system are not aligned.

Table 3.1 provides a statistical description of the autonomous health care system (HMO only), as reported by the 1994, Marion Merrell Dow (MMD) *Managed Care Digest Update Edition.*

According to the MMD study, IPA HMOs account for 26.2 million enrollees among 350 plus plans–about 50 percent of total managed care enrollment. Further, when considering that over 50 percent of group practice revenues were generated from FFS Medicare, FFS Medicaid, and commercial or private sources, it is reasonable to postulate that the autonomous system represents the dominant mode of payer/provider relations today.

Looking at HMO data, these plans require comparatively more expensive family premiums, yet a significant number are profitable. They do not do as good a job at managing inpatient days as other types of plans, yet exhibit the lowest rate of annual physician encounters.

From a general financial perspective, they appear to be in relatively good shape, given their median current ratio, debt to equity ratio, and a net worth per member that is second only to homogenous systems. From a medical utilization perspective, the autonomous system appears to be superior to synergistic systems in terms of physician and inpatient expenses.

The "face" of this system that the buyer (employer, employees) sees is that of the payer, as marketing is accomplished around the health insurance plan–not insurance plus medical delivery system. Effectively, from the perspective of marketing the system, providers are transparent; that is, the medical delivery system of the product is generally not leveraged in marketing or marketing communications activities.

On a theoretical basis, from the perspective of competitive differentiation and advantage in comparison to other system types, premium costs should be higher under this system, but access to and selection of physicians should be greater. This system should not be

TABLE 3.1. Statistical Overview of the Autonomous Health Care System

Membership and Growth Trends (mid '94)	1991: 18.1 million 1994: 26.2 million
# of HMOs, trends	1991: 365 1994: 352
% of total HMOs	1991: 62% 1994: 64%
% of profitable plans	84%
Average family premium Avg. of com., non-com. rates	$403.52
Average single premium Avg. of com., non-com. rates	$142.79
Hospital inpatient days/ 1,000 members	303.8 (non-Medicare)
Annual physician encounters	3.4 (non-Medicare)
Annual ambulatory visits	1.3 (non-Medicare)
Revenue PMPM	$111.84 (non-Medicare)
Median Current Ratio	1992: 1.17 1993: 1.13
Median Debt-Equity Ratio	1992: 2.1 1993: 1.78
Net worth/member	1992: $104 1993: $130
Return on net worth	1992: 47% 1993: 34%
Median physician service expenses	1992: $423.50 1993: $390.50
Inpatient expenses	1992: $318.50 1993: $289.50
Compensation expenses	1992: $61.00 1993: $59.50
Marketing expenses	1992: $21.25 1993: $16.50
Assets/member	$497
Return on assets	19.6%

Reported statistics for small (<50k members) and large (>50k members) were averaged for purposes of this table.

Source for the data in this table: Marion Merrell Dow, *Managed Care Digest Update Edition*, "HMO Cost Analysis and Midyear Enrollment Update," 1994.

as adept at managing cost and utilization as relationships between payers and providers are looser and reimbursement is generally in the form of some kind of discounted Fee for Service. In many markets, the marketability of the autonomous system–for purposes of developing payer/provider relationships–is dependent upon the looseness of the relationship and a FFS reimbursement, since less is given up in the way of clinical autonomy and risk.

THE SYNERGISTIC HEALTH CARE SYSTEM

The synergistic health care system strives to align the financial incentives, and combine payers and independent integrated delivery networks in a manner where their concerted actions and operations have the effect of producing outcomes that could not be realized by each participant acting independently. This *synergy* should create strong, competitive advantage over the autonomous system, as alignment of incentives should produce a commonality of certain goals and objectives that will drive costs down and favorable outcomes up. Figure 3.3 presents a graphic overview of the synergistic health care system.

Using Marion Merrell Dow data in Table 3.2 (1992,1993,1994), it appears that the synergistic system underperforms other systems from a number of perspectives. They represent the least number of managed care enrollees, have the fewest number of plans, and have the lowest percentage of profitable plans.

Taken as an average of all plans, this systems' premiums–both family and single are the highest, and their revenue per member per month is the lowest. Synergistic plans also carry the highest debt to equity ratio, and have the lowest net worth per member and return on net worth. From a medical expense perspective, the synergistic system fares no better. Physician services and inpatient expenses are the highest of all plan types, as are its compensation expenses.

These low performance indicators correspond to low participation by providers in integrated delivery networks at this point in time. They indicate that currently, the state of integration is immature, and even upon integration, financial incentives are unaligned, thus creating high costs and premiums. However, given the flurry of

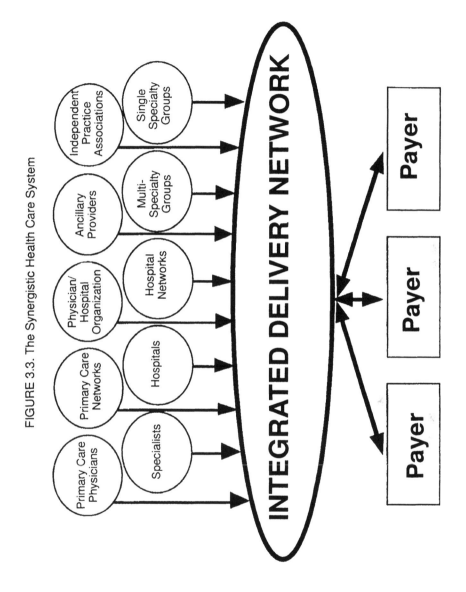

FIGURE 3.3. The Synergistic Health Care System

TABLE 3.2. Statistical Overview of the Synergistic Health Care System

Membership and Growth Trends (mid '94)	1991: 6.4 million 1994: 6.7 million
# of HMOs, trends	1991: 84 1994: 72
% of total HMOs	1991: 14% 1994: 13%
% of profitable plans	80.5%
Average family premium Avg. of community and non-community rates	$403.62
Average single premium Avg. of community and non-community rates	$152.22
Hospital inpatient days/1,000 members (non-Medicare)	289.9
Annual physician encounters (non-Medicare)	3.8
Annual ambulatory visits (non-Medicare)	1.2
Revenue PMPM (non-Medicare)	$110.35
Median Current Ratio	1992: 1.11 1993: 1.06
Median Debt/Equity Ratio	1992: 2.18 1993: 1.96
Net worth/member	1992: $119 1993: $120
Return on net worth	1992: 47% 1993: 33.5
Median physician service expenses	1992: $438.5 1993: $450.50
Inpatient expenses	1992: $379.50 1993: $351.00
Compensation expenses	1992: $58.5 1993: $86.00
Marketing expenses	1992: $21 1993: $25
Assets/member	$727
Return on assets	15.9%

Reported statistics for small (<50k members) and large (>50k members) were averaged for purposes of this table.

Source for the data in this table: Marion Merrell Dow, *Managed Care Digest Update Edition*, "HMO Cost Analysis and Midyear Enrollment Update," 1994.

integration activities, particularly as managed care penetration increases, and as IDNs increasingly take capitated reimbursement, it would not be unreasonable to expect that network model HMOs become very competitive with other models. Consequently, for the provider, a key strategic marketing issue will center around whether to join or form an IDN which in turn will involve balancing questions of current competitive disadvantages with future projections of market share based upon evolution of the market from a managed care perspective.

In this system, the payer retains external marketing responsibilities and serves as direct conduit to the customer in terms of sales and service. However, unlike the autonomous system, the composition of the medical delivery system–who participates in delivering medical benefits–may be a critical part of the payer's marketing communication's platform. In fact, identification of participating IDNs can be the basis for both product differentiation (i.e., a product delivered around a specific IDN) or around differentiation of the system as a whole. This is not to say that IDNs will have an exclusive relationship with a payer; rather, it is highly likely that most IDNs in a given market will have multiple payer relationships, since exclusivity may lead to a loss of market share. It consequently behooves the IDN to seek multiple relationships.

The synergistic health care system requires a very complex and sophisticated three-step marketing process requiring the involvement of two different sets of marketers–those on the medical side and those on the payer side. For example, as shown in Figure 3.4, marketers in a medical delivery or provider environment must participate in selecting and securing medical delivery participants for

FIGURE 3.4. Three-Step IDN Marketing Process

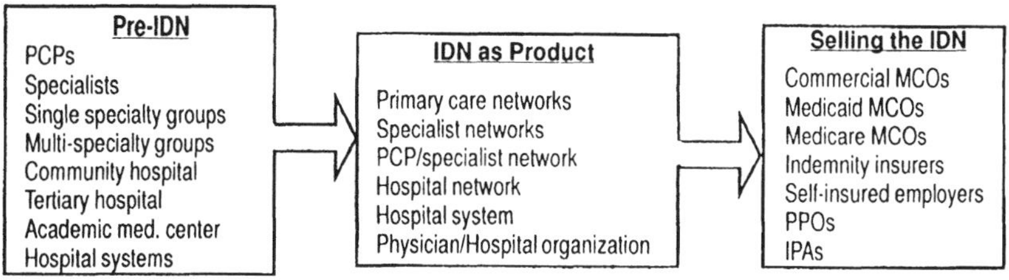

Pre-IDN	**IDN as Product**	**Selling the IDN**
PCPs		Commercial MCOs
Specialists	Primary care networks	Medicaid MCOs
Single specialty groups	Specialist networks	Medicare MCOs
Multi-specialty groups	PCP/specialist network	Indemnity insurers
Community hospital	Hospital network	Self-insured employers
Tertiary hospital	Hospital system	PPOs
Academic med. center	Physician/Hospital organization	IPAs
Hospital systems		

creating an integrated delivery system, including the creation of programs to ensure physician loyalty. Once created, the IDN must be "sold" to payers.

Developing the integrated medical delivery network will thus involve a marketing and sales process to multiple target markets (physicians and hospitals) to secure participation, and in order to achieve this goal, the network in and by itself must be marketable. In this case, marketability involves a complex set of interactions, for example: use of competitive intelligence for positioning purposes; aligning the objectives and self interests of physician and hospital "prospects"; and creating a differentiated product–an IDN responsive to customer (payer) needs–particularly in larger markets where payers may enjoy the luxury of selecting from a number of IDNs with whom to contract.

The complexities of marketing and selling the IDN to payers go beyond identification of composition and geographic distribution of the IDN. The IDN's marketing platform must include financial elements–in particular, risk-sharing agreements–which provides an opportunity to position the IDN as more of a partner than vendor, as a consequence of a willingness to develop a relationship based upon an understanding of the importance of the connection between financial results and clinical outcomes.

The process of developing and selling an IDN involves a number of strategic marketing issues which, it might be argued, fall outside of the traditional roles and responsibilities of the marketer within a medical delivery environment. Taking the perspective that the IDN is a product, however, creates a twist in the sense that like any product the IDN can be positioned, packaged, priced, and promoted. It will compete for contracts, and consequently, must be differentiated from competitors. What this suggests is that even though strategic initiatives may originate and be managed at CEO or CFO levels of the medical delivery organization, the ability to view needs and objectives from a marketing perspective will add new dimensions to the organization's ability to achieve its goals.

Once the IDN is sold to payers, the combined payer/provider alliance (the system) must be sold to end users, as shown in Figure 3.5, via processes that differentiate the system and its products from competitive systems.

FIGURE 3.5. From IDN to Payer Target Markets

Such differentiation might occur around the ability to deliver lower premiums, yet good access to physicians. Or, it might occur around the network–rather than independent–relationships between the payer and providers. Because incentives between payer and provider should come into increasing alignment under this system, it should be able to control costs, utilization, and expenses better than an autonomous system.

THE HOMOGENOUS HEALTH CARE SYSTEM

The homogenous health care system is an organizational entity where insurance and medical delivery functions are combined under one corporate identity. Here, providers deliver services exclusively to the entity, creating an environment where (theoretically) financial incentives are in complete alignment, and responsibility for outcomes–both financial and clinical–are decentralized throughout the organization. Figure 3.6 provides a graphic representation of this type of system.

The product being sold by the homogenous health care system is neither insurance nor medical delivery alone; rather, it is a combination of the two blended in a manner such that the system's medical delivery components work hand in hand with medical management, administrative, financial management, and marketing functions to deliver a product that is differentiated around brand identity and the composition of the system's medical delivery components.

According to the Marion Merrell Dow study (see Table 3.3), on the average, homogenous systems (herein defined as both Staff and Group Model HMOs) outperform other systems from a number of

FIGURE 3.6. The Homogenous Health Care System

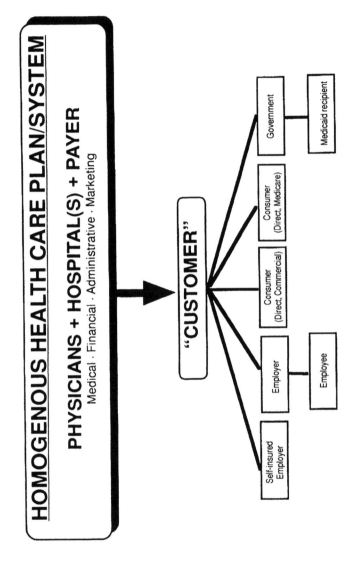

TABLE 3.3. Statistical Overview of the Homogenous Health Care System

Membership and Growth Trends (mid '94)	1991: 15.8 million 1994: 19.4 million
# of HMOs, trends	1991: 132 1994: 122
% of total HMOs	1991: 22.5% 1994: 22.3%
% of profitable plans	85.5%
Average family premium Avg. of community and non-community rates	$387.48
Average single premium Avg. of community and non-community rates	$140.76
Hospital inpatient days/1,000 members (non-Medicare)	285.5
Annual physician encounters (non-Medicare)	3.85
Annual ambulatory visits (non-Medicare)	1.7
Revenue PMPM (non-Medicare)	$113.33
Median Current Ratio	1992: 1.1 1993: .95
Median Debt/Equity Ratio	1992: 2.08 1993: 1.51
Net worth/member	1992: $120.20 1993: $131.50
Return on net worth	1992: 33.3% 1993: 334.5%
Median physician service expenses	1992: $265.50 1993: $329.70
Inpatient expenses	1992: $284.75 1993: $283.00
Compensation expenses	1992: $49.25 1993: $49.75
Marketing expenses	1992: $18.25 1993: $22.50
Assets/member	$552
Return on assets	15.7%

Reported statistics for small (<50k members) and large (>50k members) were averaged for purposes of this table. Reported statistics for Homogenous represent average of Group and Staff HMO data.

Source for the data in this table: Marion Merrell Dow, *Managed Care Digest Update Edition*, "HMO Cost Analysis and Midyear Enrollment Update," 1994.

perspectives. Although they rank second in terms of enrollees and number of plans, the highest percentage of profitable plans are homogenous, and they earn the highest revenue per member per month of any system type.

They have the lowest debt to equity ratio, and the highest net worth per member and return on net worth. Homogenous systems, as might be expected, are lowest in terms of both physician, inpatient, and compensation expenses. In terms of hospital inpatient days, these types of plans/systems outperform their counterparts. Perhaps as a consequence of their inpatient success, however, homogenous systems perform worst in terms of physician utilization both in terms of physician encounters and ambulatory visits.

The system's homogeneity becomes, in effect, an opportunity to create a shared organizational culture, and commonality of mission, goals, and values throughout the organization. It also represents an opportunity to create competitive differentiation, as customers become aware of the combination of insurance and medical delivery under one roof.

On a theoretical basis, from the perspective of competitive differentiation and advantage in comparison to other system types, the homogenous system should be able to deliver lowest premium cost, but is the most restrictive plan in terms of access and participation of physicians. This system *should* be the most adept at managing cost and utilization as relationships between payers and providers are the tightest and reimbursement is generally in the form of some kind of capitation. Table 3.4 provides a summary overview of the characteristics of the three different types of healthcare systems.

REFERENCE NOTES

1. John D. Blair, PhD, et al., "Strategic Stakeholder Management" in *MGM Journal* (May/June 1995), pp. 17-21.
2. Ibid.

TABLE 3.4. Characteristics of the Three Health Care Systems

	Autonomous	Synergistic	Homogenous
Description	• Combination of payer and autonomous, independent physicians and hospitals • Marketing accomplished around health insurance plan, not insurance plus medical delivery—basically, the payer is the "system" • Financial incentives for acting as a unified whole are not aligned • Physicians may be grouped (i.e., IPA, group practices) • Physicians and hospitals may have multiple contractual relationships with payers • From marketing perspective, providers are transparent to customers—i.e., composition of medical delivery system not used as a marketing tool; customer recognition of payers only	• Combination of payer and independent intertwined delivery networks • Two types of marketing functions required: one to create IDNs (internal); one to secure enrollment (external) • External marketing effected at payer level only; customer awareness relates "system" to payer • Financial incentives increasingly come into alignment, creating synergy—where combined, concerted actions/operations have the effect of producing outcomes that could not be realized by each participant acting independently • IDNs may have multiple, risk-based contractual relationships with payers • Composition of medical delivery system becomes a critical part of marketing communications platform; basis for differentiation	• Combination of payer and providers in one organized entity • Providers are exclusive to payers • Staff and group model IMOs • Financial incentives in complete alignment; responsibility for outcomes of all types decentralized throughout organization • Theoretically, system represents best type of structure for controlling utilization • Blending of payer and provider creates homogeneity relative to organizational culture, mission, goals, objectives • Homogeneity becomes basis for competitive differentiation; customer is aware of both insurance and medical delivery combination
Marketing function	Resident at payer	Resident at payer—external Resident at MD and hospital—internal	Resident at health care plan/system
(Theoretical) Factors for Competitive Differentiation and Advantage	Product: *insurance* Payer provider relationship: *loose* Incentives: *unaligned* Reimbursement: *mostly some form of FFS* Patient access: *best* Premium costs: *higher* System ability to control costs: *worst* System ability to control utilization: *worst* System ability to achieve economies of scale: *worst* "Face" that buyer sees: *payer*	Product: *insurance and medical delivery* Payer provider relationship: *tighter* Incentive: *aligning* Reimbursement: *capitation and some forms of FFS* Patient access: *good* Premium costs: *high* System ability to control costs: *better* System ability to control utilization: *better* System ability to achieve economies of scale: *better* "Face" that buyer sees: *payer and medical delivery*	Product: *insurance/medical delivery* Payer provider relationship: *tightest* Incentive: *aligned* Reimbursement: *capitation* Patient access: *worst* Premium costs: *lower* System ability to control costs: *best* System ability to control utilization: *best* System ability to achieve economies of scale: *best* "Face" that buyer sees: *health care system*

TABLE 3.4 (continued)

	Internal (pre-IDN)	Internal (post-IDN)	External	Patients
Health Care System's Target Markets	Employers and employees not self-insured	PCPs Specialists Single specialty groups Multi-specialty groups Primary care networks Specialist networks PCP/specialist network Community hospital Tertiary hospital Academic med. center Hospital network Hospital system	Commercial MCOs Medicaid MCOs Medicare MCOs Indemnity insurers Self-insured employers PPOs IPAs	Self-insured employers Employers (commercial) Employees Business coalitions Medicare eligibles Medicaid eligibles	Self-insured employers Employers (commercial) Employees Business coalitions Medicare eligibles Medicaid eligibles
Membership and Growth Trends (mid '94)	1991: 18.1 million 1994: 26.2 million	1991: 6.4 million 1994: 6.7 million		1991: 15.8 million 1994: 19.4 million
# of HMOs, trends	1991: 365 1994: 352	1991: 84 1994: 72		1991: 132 1994: 122
% of total HMOs	1991: 62% 1994: 64%	1991: 14% 1994: 13%		1991: 22.5% 1994: 22.3%
% of profitable plans	84%	80.5%		85.5%
Average family premium	$403.52	$403.62		$387.48
Average single premium	$142.79	$152.22		$140.76

Hospital inpatient days/1,000 members (non-Medical)	303.8	289.9	285.5
Annual MD encounters (non-Medicare)	3.4	3.8	3.85
Annual ambulatory visits (non-Med)	1.3	1.2	1.7
Revenue PMPM (non-Medicare)	$111.84	$110.35	
Median Current Ratio	1992: 1.17 1993: 1.13	1992: 1.11 1993: 1.06	1992: 1.1 1993: .95
Median Debt/Equity	1992: 2.10 1993: 1.78	1992: 2.18 1993: 1.96	1992: 2.08 1993: 1.51
Net worth/member	1992: $104 1993: $130	1992: $119 1993: $120	1992: $120.20 1993: $131.50
Return on net worth	1992: 47% 1993: 34%	1992: 47% 1993: 33.5%	1992: 33.3% 1993: 34.5%
Median MD service expenses	1992: $423.50 1993: $390.50	1992: $438.50 1993: $450.50	1992: $265.50 1993: $329.70
Inpatient expenses	1992: $318.50 1993: $289.50	1992: $379.50 1993: $351.00	1992: $284.75 1993:$283.00
Compensation expenses	1992: $61.00 1993: $59.50	1992: $58.50 1993: $86.00	1992: $49.25 1993: $49.75
Marketing expenses	1992: $21.25 1993: $16.50	1992: $21 1993: $25	1992: $18.25 1993: $22.50
Assets/member	$497	$727	$552
Return on assets	19.6%	15.9%	15.7%

Reported statistics for small (50k members) and large (<50k members) were averaged for purpose of this table. Reported statistics for Homogenous represent average of Group and Staff HMO data.

Source for the data in this table: Marion Merrell Dow, *Managed Care Digest Update Edition*, "HMO Cost Analysis and Midyear Enrollment Update," 1994.

CHAPTER 4:
WINNING THE WAR–CRITICAL
FACTORS FOR SUCCESS
IN THE CHANGING DYNAMIC

The marketer is a professional whose basic interest and skill lies in regulating the level, timing, and character of demand for a product, service, place, or idea. If demand is negative, it must be disabused; if non-existent, it must be created; if latent, it must be developed; if faltering, it must be revitalized; if irregular, it must be synchronized; if full, it must be maintained; if overfull, it must be reduced; and finally, if unwholesome, it must be destroyed.

–Philip Kotler, "The Major Tasks
of Marketing Management" in
The Journal of Marketing, Vol. 37 (October 1973)

The other day, while perusing *The New York Times*, I ran across an advertisement placed by an organization named Code Blue. Without holding any punches, the ad was a blatant attack on managed care, citing a number of reasons why managed care is horrific in concept and practice. Intrigued, I called the organization and requested an information package, which, sad to say, has yet to grace my mailbox.

However, what Code Blue did for me was to reaffirm, albeit in a vituperative manner, that although managed care has achieved phenomenal growth, some 200 million Americans are not managed care members. They also made me think that regardless of health care system or type of insurance they are based upon, each system has the responsibility to create awareness and drive preferential purchase decisions. At the health care system level, the result of awareness and preference is enrollment, which is the key to the success of the system and an indication of its viability for participants.

In the changing dynamic, the responsibility for creating awareness and driving preference does not belong to the payer or health care system alone. Providers too must assume responsibility, as their ability to create awareness of who they are and what they do represent the basis for contracting, integration, and integrated delivery network opportunities. For example, in a synergistic system, IDN organizers must create awareness of the IDN and drive providers to join. Once formed, the IDN as an organization must assume responsibility for creating awareness of its existence among payers and/or employers, followed by securing a relationship (driving the purchase decision).

SEEKING AND SECURING
COMPETITIVE ADVANTAGE

There can be little doubt that the health care industry is in the midst of a protracted war. Cost pressures are changing clinical, administrative, and financial relationships between and among payers, physicians, and hospitals. Managed care penetration is growing, spurred by employer demands for value and accountability. The health care market is being localized, yet nationally based companies are committing enormous resources to ensure their presence at the local level. Providers, seeking to protect market share and income, are scrambling to join or form integrated delivery networks and managed care organizations.

And through it all, payers, physicians, and hospitals are aligning into different types of health systems to compete against one another in different types of evolving markets.

From a marketer's perspective, however, there are a critical set of factors which, acting in concert with one another, have the ability to create long-term, sustainable competitive advantage for any type of health care system combat on in any type of health care battlefield. But what is competitive advantage and why is it so important? Why should payers, physicians, and hospitals care about competitive advantage? What does it take to create and sustain competitive advantage?

Competitive advantage is a spirit, a behavior, a desire to win and to be the very best at what you do. It is reflected in the attitudes and demeanor of employees, from the mail room clerk to the CEO. It is an integral part of the essence and character of an organization, reflected in the quality of its services and products, in a belief in its services and products, and in the aggressiveness and willingness of employees to promote and sell the organization internally and externally.

Competitive advantage involves a willingness to aggressively fight for market share and position, for continually increasing sales, and for establishing irrevocable and unbreakable linkages between the organization and its customers. Creating a competitive advantage requires a commitment in terms of time, resources, thinking, and behavior to consistently outmaneuver competitors. And when accomplished, competitive advantage leads to both tangible, measurable outcomes ranging from fantastic sales to phenomenal return to shareholders and/or stakeholders; and intangible outcomes, such as pride, motivation, and a gut level, fundamental feeling that you are the very best at what you do.

Competitive advantage requires a willingness to capitalize upon strengths of the organization and weaknesses of competitors. It means seizing opportunities or making opportunities to grow a category or drive preference. It involves an ability to recognize and respond to threats before they become a damaging force. The desire for competitive advantage lies at the very core of the organization.

Some payers, physician organizations, and hospital organizations–mostly those for profit–have recognized the value of competitive advantage and are driving the dynamics of the health care industry. Companies like U.S. Healthcare, Oxford, Phycor, Columbia/HCA, and many others have bulldozed through market entry barriers and have carried the concept of competitive advantage to the point where established health care systems are put in the position of *reacting* to their presence, rather than *proactively* seeking to create and sustain their own competitive advantage.

All too often, the cry of health care altruism is raised as a shield against competitive advantage. "After all," many providers and not-for-profit payers exclaim, "We're in the business of serving the health needs of our community. We can't be concerned about business and marketing and all that stuff. . . . I didn't go to Medical School (or Graduate School or Law School) to become a salesperson!"

Perhaps the best reason I ever heard for seeking and securing competitive advantage occurred in a free-wheeling discussion my partner and I had with a group of physicians who were tying to decide whether or not to organize into a risk-bearing physician's organization. The debate raged on hour after hour, with some physicians taking the position that the new organization should be an HMO, while others passionately pleaded that physicians are healers, not businessmen, and should not even be considering a new organization. Finally, one doctor (an optometrist) spoke up.

"Fellows," he said, "Here's why we have to take the initiative and do something . . . IF WE DON'T DO IT, IT'S GONNA BE DONE FOR US AND TO US!!!"

The debate ended at that point. To those who believe that the concept of health care is and must forever be separate from the business and marketing of health care, be prepared to have "it" done to you or for you.

Competitive advantage in the health care industry is a combination of entrepreneurship and medicine, such that the delivery and financing of health care is accomplished in a manner where financial benefits accrue to participants, and reasonably priced health care benefits (i.e., well-being) accrue to users of the health care system. Of course, it is very possible that the balance between entrepreneurism and medicine can move too far in either direction, and finding and defining the appropriate balance should lie at the core of the organization's mission or charter.

Competitive advantage is not just a function of the health care system alone. Providers too can seek and create competitive advantage, from securing exclusive contracts to forcing mergers or alliances to creating integrated delivery networks as a means of organizing and leveraging provider clout.

COMPONENTS OF COMPETITIVE ADVANTAGE

The ability to create, secure, and sustain competitive advantage involves the interaction, integration, and blending of two groups or sets of activities. The internal set, labeled *Competitive Innovation* in Figure 4.1, addresses the research, planning, and positioning needs of the health care system for achieving competitive advantage and is, in effect, a key aspect of preparations necessary for going into battle. Competitive innovation is a process requiring the health care marketer's commitment and willingness to "break out of the box" of conventional thinking and norms. The practice of competitive innovation involves re-evaluating and rethinking what health care plans/systems are, what they do, and their fundamental meaning and value to both participants and customers. Competitive innovation culminates in the development of unconventional products, new ways of delivering and marketing existing products, and even new mutually beneficial organizational relationships and structures.

The external set of activities, labeled *Market Excitation* in Figure 4.1, represents those activities that are *directly* involved in fighting the battle, that is, creating awareness and driving preference. These external activities are called Market Excitation because winning competitive advantage is exciting, and the process of achieving desirable outcomes should energize and invigorate the organization.

The need for Market Excitation applies equally as well to providers seeking to market services to a payer as they do to physicians and hospitals seeking to form an integrated delivery network, or to the health care system seeking enrollment. From customer service to marketing communications, Market Excitation activities represent the "front line" of the organization to its prospects and customers, and create the environment and conditions for winning competitive advantage.

Together–and only together–will these components create com-

FIGURE 4.1. Critical Factors for Success

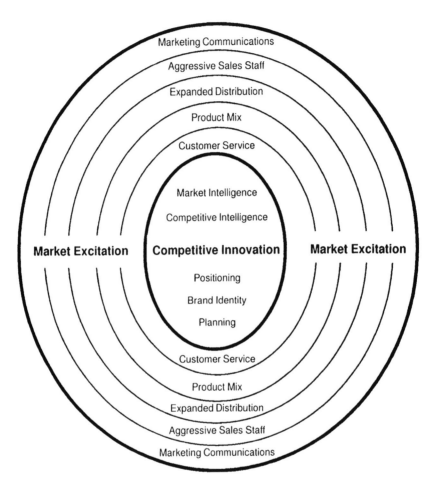

petitive advantage and ultimately win the battle for security, prosperity, and autonomy. They are integrally and fundamentally interconnected, and only when working in concert with one another can competitive advantage be produced. For example, marketing communications without differentiated positioning is valueless, or expanding a product mix without competitive intelligence is folly. The art and process of competitive innovation and market excitation are discussed in the following chapters.

CHAPTER 5:
PREPARING FOR BATTLE–
THE ART AND PROCESS
OF COMPETITIVE INNOVATION

But I'm coming to believe that all of us are ghosts. . . . It's not just what we inherit from our mothers and fathers. It's also the shadows of dead ideas and opinions and convictions. They're no longer alive, but they grip us all the same, and hold on to us against our will. . . . They are haunting the whole country, those stubborn phantoms–so many of them, so thick, they're like an impenetrable dark mist. And here we are, all of us, so abjectly terrified of the light.

–Henrik Ibsen, *Ghosts*

As shown in Figure 5.1, competitive innovation is the foundation upon which the health care system prepares for battle. It is an integral and fundamental element for turning the chaos of the changing dynamic into opportunity. Without a commitment to competitive innovation–both in terms of behavior and resources–the health care system will end up being driven by the market, rather than being a driver of the market.

On the battlefield of the changing dynamic, the ability of a health

FIGURE 5.1. Competitive Innovation as a Foundation for Competitive Advantage

care system to seize and maintain a competitive advantage in its market will be directly related to its capacity for competitive innovation. Currently, too many organizations expend enormous energy simply to reproduce cost, benefit, administrative, or service advantages their competitors already enjoy. The system, guided by a competitive innovation demeanor, will seek to capitalize upon the unique strengths or abilities of the organization as it currently exists, or to create new capabilities driven by market need, or to evolve to an organizational structure more responsive to battlefield conditions.

As managed care penetration increases, health care marketers must drive their organizations to becoming competitive innovators by addressing a combination of factors that ultimately will determine their viability in the marketplace: competitive intent, strategy, and tactics; customer psychographics and demographics; marketplace trends; customer desires and needs; the organization's strengths, weaknesses, and resources; and barriers to innovation.

Throughout this book it has been strongly suggested that the changing dynamic is a war zone characterized by transition or shift—in terms of dollars, enrollment, and power—as managed care penetration increases and indemnity enrollment decreases within local markets. While some systems need not do anything more than ensure that they have an adequate distribution channel (i.e., representation at the employer level) in order to capture dollars or subscribers/members in transition, competitive innovators will become market driven, aggressively capitalize upon opportunities, and develop the means to maintain their gains.

These transitions are creating opportunities for new ways of defining who or what "a customer" is; for creating value-added products or services; for expanding value chains; for seeking new distribution channels; and for creating medical delivery systems, marketing innovations, administrative systems, and alignments of financial and clinical interests that will convince current subscribers/members to remain loyal to a system and induce or motivate prospects to a favorable purchase decision. Understanding the dynamics of these shifts and capitalizing upon them are the breeding grounds for competitive innovation and the marketing battleground of the 1990s and beyond for the health care industry.

Competitive innovation is a way of thinking, a behavior, a commitment on behalf of both payer and provider participants within a health care system to fulfilling the plan's vision by seeking and securing competitive advantages in the service areas in which it operates. Competitive innovation is thus a foundation of competitive advantage, the forerunner of strategic planning, and a building block for market excitement.

The goal of competitive innovation is not necessarily to become the market's leader; rather, its objective is to deliver leverageable, market-driven programs, products, and services (at best, not offered by competitors) and in the process, create growth, income, and the sustained satisfaction and loyalty of subscriber/members, employers, and participants. While the effects of innovation may result in share gain, its true measure is reflected in the system's ability to either create or enlarge the scope of its competitive advantages–not only by reacting to trends but also serving as a catalyst to create trends.

Competitive innovation is built upon a deep understanding of the system's external and internal operating environments, ranging from demographic trends to comprehensive competitor analysis to policy and procedural analyses. It involves knowing the market, its future, and the desires/needs of customers, as well as the position and status of the system in the market. For the market leader, it means not sitting on laurels but protecting or enhancing their position by capitalizing upon proprietary strengths and competitor's weaknesses, and for other players in the market, it means filling gaps not addressed by the leader in a financially responsible manner.

Competitive innovation will not be successful and competitive advantage cannot be created if the health care marketer does not hear or listen to "the voice of the market." Hearing the market's voice involves both statistical and perceptual analyses of customers, participant "prospects," and competitors. Listening to the voice of the market involves understanding the meaning of this data, particularly in terms of its use for creating competitive advantage.

Competitive innovation can lead to income sanctuaries–uncontested places in the market uniquely suited to the system's current strengths or appropriate for developing a strength. Finding these sanctuaries begins with a determination to create value for both participants and customers while trying to avoid competition.

Efforts to create value for customers may in fact involve a redefinition of what a customer is and a reevaluation of how to best organize medical delivery, marketing, sales, administrative, and relational resources to meet their needs and expectations. Consider, for example, that a customer can be an industry, a current account, an employer prospect, a subscriber, a member, a consumer prospect, or Medicaid or Medicare eligibles. Competitive innovation thus involves a process of analyzing purchase behaviors, motivations, and the objectives, goals, and values which motivate customers to preferential action.

Achieving competitive advantage through innovation is not an overnight process or a one time/one shot effort given the dynamic nature of health care marketing. The essence of competitive innovation lies in an ability to create tomorrow's competitive advantages faster than competitor's mimic the ones the system possesses today. Bringing innovations to fruition involves development of a long range view of market needs, a plan to respond to those needs, and the resolution to expend resources in a responsible manner. As shown in Figure 5.2, the process of competitive information involves three key steps:

1. Hearing the voice of the market,
2. Listening to the voice of the market, and
3. Responding to the voice of the market.

HEARING AND LISTENING
TO THE VOICE OF THE MARKET

The phrase "knowledge is power," first used by Sir Francis Bacon in 1597, was used in the context of the sixteenth-century view that knowledge is the power through which mankind can create a better life here on earth. Bacon's premise, that the power of knowledge is a resource that enables other things to happen, is fundamental to the process of competitive innovation. Barabba and Zaltman, in their landmark book *Hearing the Voice of the Market* (1991), amplify this statement by focusing on the belief that even

FIGURE 5.2. The Process of Competitive Innovation

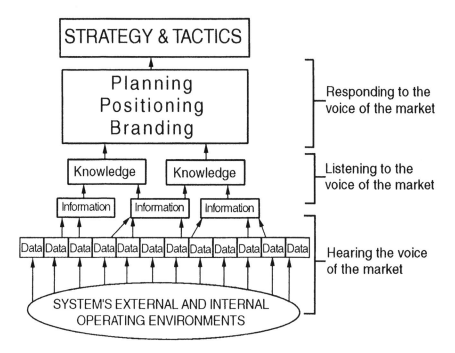

small improvements in learning about the marketplace and in making creative use of marketing information can have a major effect in eliciting more favorable responses to a company's offering.

The first step in the process of competitive innovation, hearing the voice of the market, is an expensive and time-consuming part of any effort leading to competitive advantage. Upon completion, this step will help health care marketers know what their market is all about—who the players are and their positions; what prospects and customers currently think; what prospects and customers need or want; what the service area looks like from a demographic perspective and future demographic trends; strategic innovations and moves made by competitors; and ultimately, the system's strengths, weaknesses, opportunities, and threats in the internal and external environment in which they operate. Table 5.1 provides a partial

TABLE 5.1. Types of Data Necessary for Hearing the Voice of the Market

(1) Population demographics
- total; age/sex; education; HH income; growth/decline trends; seasonal variations

(2) Insurance environment
- under 65 insured: total, managed care, indemnity, self-funded
- Medicare
- Medicaid
- uninsured

(3) Business environment including employers and employment
- local economy characteristics and projections
- total employed, employment by type of employer
- total companies: < 100; 100-499; 500-999; >1,000
- top 50 employers
- # self-funded employers; number of employees covered

(4) Payer environment
- system characteristics, strategy
- Indemnity: company, penetration, medical delivery system characteristics, strategy
- integration activities

(5) Utilization statistics and trends
- market's health care costs
- hospital care costs
- utilization: physician services
- utilization: inpatient services
- utilization: ancillary services

(6) Physician environment
- # physicians: total and per thousand
- PCPs (solo, group, academic, affiliated, non-affiliated)
- specialists (solo, group, academic, affiliated, non-affiliated)
- PCP trends
- integration activities

(7) Employer perspectives
- Focus groups
- One-on-one interviews
- Perceptions of competitors
- Price sensitivity studies
- Re-positioning
- Advertising awareness

(8) Hospital perspectives
- Perception of plan administration
- Perception of plan communications
- Perception of fee/reimbursement
- Perception of medical policies
- Member education issues
- Competition's panel and distribution
- Competition's fee and fee schedule
- Competition's administrative policies
- Competition's medical policies

(9) Physician perspectives
- Perception of plan administration
- Perception of plan communications
- Perception of fee/reimbursement
- Perception of medical policies
- Member education issues
- Competition's panel and distribution
- Competition's fee and fee schedule
- Competition's administrative policies
- Competition's medical policies

(10) Consumer and member perspectives
- Focus groups
- In-home one-on-one interviews
- Loyalty-satisfaction issues
- Perceptions of products
- Perceptions of competitors
- Price sensitivity studies
- Re-positioning
- Advertising awareness

(11) Internal environment
- Inter- and Intra-department relationships
- Available resources
- Capabilities and capacity
- Assessment of strengths
- Assessment of weaknesses

listing of the types of data necessary for hearing the voice of the market.

While there are many different types of market research at a bare minimum, every health care marketer should know the answers to the following five questions from his/her customers: (1) Do you know who we are and what we do? (2) What do you think of us? (3) What do we stand for? (4) What do you think about our competitors? (5) What do you want or need from us, or from our competitors, that you are not now getting?

Strategic and tactical responses to the answers to these questions alone potentially represent years of competitive innovation and advantage for any health care system. All too often, the sum total of market research done by the system today is the time-worn "satisfaction survey"–a tool which generally indicates that "customers are satisfied" with the plan. These are generally done with one survey instrument to solicit feedback, and the survey is based on the plan's assumptions about what customers care about, not actual data from the customers themselves.

However, just as there is a danger from a lack of research, there is the danger of "research paralysis"–not being able to make decisions without quantifiable, statistically valid data. The key to appropriate use of market research is one of balance: too little and the health care marketer runs into the danger of not understanding and consequently not being responsive to the market; too much and the marketer runs into the danger of being unable to make decisions without more data!

All market research will do for the health care marketer is to enable him to "hear the voice of the market." Translating data into meaningful or insightful observations (listening to the voice of the market) is a wholly distinct activity requiring a combination of intuition and creativity. The difference between hearing the voice of the market and listening to the voice is the difference between data/information and knowledge.

As data is collected, its usefulness must be assessed, but more importantly, its meaning must be assessed. Table 5.2 shows some examples of questions that turn data into knowledge.

One of the most critical elements of hearing the voice of the market is competitive intelligence. Sun Tzu, the masterful Chinese

TABLE 5.2. From Data to Knowledge

Marketplace Statistics	• What demographic trends or shifts are occurring that we should be sensitive to? • Does the distribution of employers by size adequately correspond to the organization of our sales force? • Should we pursue a category growth strategy, a drive preference strategy, or some combination?
Market Share Statistics	• At both the employer and employee level, what is the rate of shift away from indemnity plans, and how can we best capitalize upon that shift? • Have any of our competitors achieved a rapid rise in share, and if so, why?
Consumer/ Member Perspectives	• Are consumer/member perspectives of our plan where we want them to be, and if not, why not? • How effective is our marketing communications program in terms of establishing our position? Enrolling new members? Changing perceptions? • What benefit/cost/provider access/image changes are necessary for motivating prospects to switch?
Employer Perspectives	• Are we meeting employer's needs or expectations, and if not, why not? • What are the barriers preventing us from acquiring new accounts or increasing penetration within existing accounts? • Is our marketing communications budget against employers, particularly in relation to spending against consumers, adequate?
Provider Perspectives	• How much influence do providers have in terms of convincing members to switch plans? • Is provider dissatisfaction affecting our marketing goals, and if so, how?
Competitor Analysis	• What is the strategic intent of our competitors and how is its execution impacting us? • How are competitors attempting to differentiate, and how meaningful is that differentiation from consumer and employer perspectives? • What weaknesses do our competitors have that we can capitalize upon?
Internal Environment	• Are our administrative, policy, procedural, or technological capabilities adequate for accomplishing our strategic intent? • Are inter- and intra-departmental relationships focused upon realizing our vision?

military strategist, wrote in *The Art of War* that, ". . . if you know others and know yourself, you will not be imperiled in a hundred battles; if you do not know others but know yourself, you win one and lose one; if you do not know others and do not know yourself, you will be imperiled in every single battle."

A fundamental key to competitive innovation lies in a sound, well-maintained competitive intelligence program. Knowing the competition is not a particularly difficult task, especially in an industry governed by regulatory reporting requirements. Annual financial and "data requirement" reports provide a wealth of information regarding current structure, market share, and strategic intent; HMO rate filings provide insights to competitive premium development processes; collateral materials often reveal positioning and communications platforms; and even public hearings can provide information as to how a competitor will be approaching the market and his intent.

Minimally, each health care system should know the following about its competition:

- products, riders, costs;
- statistical position in the marketplace (market share, share of voice, etc.) by customer;
- operational statistics;
- medical utilization statistics;
- medical delivery system composition;
- how it is perceived by consumers (customers and prospects);
- how it is perceived by employers (customers and prospects);
- how it is perceived by physicians (participants, prospects, non-participants);
- how it is perceived by hospitals (participants, prospects, non-participants);
- financial condition, including expenditures by category;
- marketing communications expenditures;
- marketing and advertising campaigns.

The net effect of gathering and analyzing this information is that the health care marketer will gain an understanding of the competition's strengths and weaknesses and the threats they pose, creating an opportunity to develop both proactive and reactive strategies or tactics. Competitive analysis provides the means for defining strategic opportunities for long-term growth, new product opportunities, and ways to capitalize upon competitive weaknesses.

RESPONDING TO THE VOICE
OF THE MARKET–POSITIONING AND PLANNING

The final step in the process of competitive innovation is *responding* to the voice of the market. While there are a variety of planning formats for formalizing the health care system's drive for competitive innovation, at a minimum, four key questions must be answered:

1. Based upon what we know about our internal and external environment, where are the viable opportunities for either making or seizing a competitive advantage?

While many systems may be tactically proficient, their lack of competitive advantage may be a function of an indiscernible position in their market. Perhaps the two most critical questions faced by the system's marketing and sales department are, "What makes you different from your competitors?" and "Why should I buy your product?"

Positioning a health care system is perhaps one of the most critical elements for achieving long-term, sustainable growth. Not only should it strive to be different from its competitors, but also, it must strive to make sure that such differences are meaningful to both purchasers and participants. One might argue, in fact, that health care systems cannot afford a single position and because of the nature of the competitive and sales environment, at least three different types of positions are necessary: a business-to-business position (employers) and a consumer position, each of which incorporates both category (managed care vs. indemnity) and competitive (plan vs. plan) differentiation; and a position directed to medical delivery participants, because like employers and consumers, they need to be "sold" (i.e., recruited) and retained.

Integrated Delivery Networks, too, should consider positioning on multiple levels as it will also have multiple targets. For example, one

MSO based in the Northeast that we worked with felt that it needed a position for three targets: physician participants, payers, and investors. Their positioning statements are presented in Table 5.3.

In fact, Michael Porter talks about five competitive forces–the threat of new entrants; the bargaining power of suppliers; rivalry among existing firms; the threats of substitute products or services; and the bargaining power of buyers–that determine the strength of competitive forces, maintaining that "the goal of competitive strategy . . . is to find a position in the industry where the company can best defend itself against these competitive forces or can influence them in its favor."[1] Porter also maintains that this is a process of taking the structure of an industry (or market) as given and match-

---

TABLE 5.3. Example of Multiple Positionings

For MDs/participants

"Our MSO is a physician-sponsored and controlled management services organization aggregating physicians' financial and clinical clout to give participants a greater share of voice in the community's health care environment. Through multiple options for participation, MSO creates the means for physicians to control their destiny, assume greater risk and realize greater financial and clinical reward, and reduce administrative burdens and costs."

For Investors

"Our MSO is a medical management services organization offering network/managed care and business administrative services to physician participants. Through a combination of differentiated products, utilization management controls created by physician participants, cost savings accrued as a result of economies of scale and multiple locations, our MSO will produce a superior return on investment."

For Payers

"Our MSO is a payer-friendly medical management services organization offering a geographically dispersed, multi-specialty (*non-branded, transparent*), managed care network. Through clinical guidelines and protocols, strict credentialing and utilization management, and administrative efficiencies, our MSO will meet payer's premium control objectives and create opportunities for developing alternative managed care products."

---

ing the company's strengths and weaknesses to it. Strategy can then be viewed as building defenses against competitive forces or as finding positions in the industry where the forces are weakest.[2]

Positioning must be correlated to the health care system's long-term strategic intent and be a reflection of sustainable growth opportunities within the framework of both the system's and its competitor's strengths and weaknesses. According to Porter, there are three broad categories for making or seizing a competitive advantage: differentiation, focus, or cost leadership. The system's strategic intent will reflect one (or possibly two) of these categories, and in effect, should characterize the organization's strategy for achieving competitive innovation.

As shown in Table 5.4, there are a wide variety of possibilities for

TABLE 5.4. Positioning Possibilities

Categories	Opportunities
Differentiation	• Market driven products • Market driven benefits • Owning or controlling components of the supply chain • Develop or target products based on demographics • Develop or target products based upon psychographics • Premium costs • Expanded product mix • Quality/service • Legal or tax status
Focus	• Develop or target products for vertical markets (i.e., industry specific) • Develop or target products for horizontal markets (i.e., Medicare) • Capture employers and employees switching from indemnity • Concentrate marketing efforts on distribution channel—employers
Cost Leadership	• Benefits rich/highest premium costs • Benefits poor/lowest premium costs • Customized benefits packages at employer's level • Premium "discounting" for volume

any health care system to achieve competitive innovation and advantage pursuant to strategic intent and positioning.

2. How leverageable are these opportunities?

Even though the system may have strengths in certain areas, or even if competitive weaknesses have been identified, or even if untouched market niche opportunities have been discovered, their usefulness from the perspective of competitive innovation and advantage must be carefully assessed.

Considerable attention must be devoted to ensuring that changes–in terms of medical delivery system composition, products, benefits, administration, and even strategic intent–are market driven rather than product or capabilities driven.

3. What changes will we have to make in order to make or seize opportunities?

Generally speaking, the process of competitive innovation involves change, perhaps in terms of policies, procedures, participation requirements, technologies, behaviors, etc., and an ability to focus both the payer and medical delivery participants on achieving the goals of change.

Once strategic intent has been defined and opportunities assessed, it is critical that a "Mission Statement" be developed that captures the strategic intent of the system in a succinct form. The Mission Statement should represent a rallying point for the organization, and in fact, serve as a criteria for decision making. Questions related to implementing specific tactical activities thus change from "Should we do it?" to "How will the implementation of this activity further our drive toward our vision?"

Mission Statements also serve as a foundation for building the actual strategic plan. It will provide the basis for creating goals (quantitative criteria for success), strategies (what the system is going to do to achieve goals), and tactics (how strategies will be accomplished).

Examples of several actual Mission Statements are presented in Table 5.5. The first, for a group model HMO, reflects the plan's orientation to health care improvements. The second, for a physician network, reflects a much more businesslike orientation, pursuant to its goal of building an integrated delivery network.

TABLE 5.5. Examples of Mission Statements

(Group Model HMO) Mission Statement

"We are dedicated to providing quality health services that are responsive to our members and accounts, and to promoting healthy lifestyles.

We are committed to fostering an environment that encourages and rewards superior service throughout our system.

We believe our mission can be accomplished best through a prepaid group practice.

We use our standing in the health care community to foster sound public policy on those issues pertaining to universal access and affordable health care."

Physician Network Mission Statement

"Our network's mission is to:

*   give physicians a greater share of voice in their market to better control their destiny;
*   access, organize, and leverage physician power to create new, mutually beneficial types of fiscal, clinical, and administrative relations with payers;
*   deliver practice level administrative and management services, providing relief from administrative burdens, and cost savings through economies of scale;
*   create benefits for the network which can be delivered back to members and the community at-large; and
*   provide a reasonable return on investment to shareholders."

---

4. What will it cost to make these changes, how will we finance them, and what sources of financing are available?

The ultimate test of achieving competitive innovation and creating competitive advantage lies in whether the system has the financial resources to make necessary changes. While for-profit systems can capitalize their needs through investors, the not-for-profit may face significant difficulties if capitalization must come out of leveraging current assets or using current reserves and future margins. Not-for-profits might consider developing holding companies with for-profit subsidiaries that will facilitate an ability to secure capitalization, or creating strategic alliances which minimize capitalization needs in consideration of shared risks and rewards.

RESPONDING TO THE VOICE OF THE MARKET–CREATING A BRAND, BRAND IDENTITY, AND BRAND EQUITY

At the Alliance for Healthcare Strategy and Marketing's 1995 Annual Conference, Eric Berkowitz, PhD, summarized the state of branding in the health care industry quite succinctly:

> Branding is kind of the ignored marketing decision. How many national brand name healthcare organizations do we have? Probably none. In healthcare, to create brand equity requires multiple factors, but to reinforce brand equity requires significant expenditures in advertising. I think that in the next five to seven years, we are going to see a level of advertising expenditures that we have never before seen in healthcare. We are going to go back to what everybody always said we are moving away from—which was defining marketing as healthcare.[3]

As markets evolve, the basis of differentiation between health care systems will evolve from category to product to brand. The health care system marketer must recognize and act upon the relationship between a market's evolutionary process and stage, and selection and execution of appropriate strategic marketing initiatives. For example, in emerging markets, particularly from the perspective of the managed care organization, marketing activities should be directed toward growing the category; that is, moving people out of indemnity coverage to managed care. In consolidating markets, while category growth is still important, strategic marketing initiatives also need to be directed toward market share growth through product differentiation, as the health care system competes for a growing pool of managed care prospects. In the mature market, where there are only a few large competitors who have the ability to quickly duplicate product innovations, market share growth becomes a function of brand differentiation.

Participants in the health care industry have done an inadequate job at establishing brand identity and accruing benefits from obtaining brand equity. In the changing dynamic, competitive innovation will be associated with those organizations that can create and grow brand identity, ultimately contributing to seizing competitive advantage. As markets evolve, and as product differentiation on the basis of benefits and costs erode, establishing brand identity and accruing brand equity will become a key component of competitive innovation. In the future, the brand will become the real capital of the health care system. Currently, the tendency in the industry is to manage products that happen to have a name.

What is a brand, and why will it become so important to achieving competitive success in the changing dynamic? Jean-Noel Kapferer, in *Strategic Brand Management*, writes:

> For the potential customer, a brand is a landmark. Like money, it facilitates trade. Faced with a multitude of silent or "hard to read" products, whose performance cannot be assessed at first glance, customers are confused. Brands and prices make products easier to "read," removing uncertainty. A product's price measures is monetary value; its brand identifies the product and reveals facets of its differences. . . . A brand encapsulates identity, origin, specificity, and difference. . . . This is why brands are vital for business exchange: when faced with say, (multitudes of choices), a buyer can use brands to structure this selection, to segment it, helping him to decide what he wants, looking toward the products whose brands indicate they will satisfy his expectations, needs or wishes. . . . Brands identify, guarantee, structure and stabilize supply. They draw their value from their capacity to reduce risk and uncertainty.[4]

Brands can segment the market and give products meaning and direction. A brand is both the memory and future of its products; to a very large degree, a brand name is a type of contract in the sense that it may reduce customers' and prospects' sense of uncertainty while achieving an almost automatic favorable opinion of any new products launched. David Arnold, in *The Handbook of Brand Management*, writes that branding has to do with the way customers buy and perceive things, and that a brand is a form of mental shorthand offering tangible benefits over and above the product. He cites that market leaders and superior brand positions are interlocked, and that market-leading brands tend to have higher profit margins.[5] Creating a brand is neither inexpensive nor quick, because brands are built up by persistent difference over time, and while product innovation is occurring on a consistent basis in the health care industry, products will live and disappear, yet a health care system brand will endure.

The process of branding a health care system can be accomplished in four steps: decide to launch a brand; create brand identity; create a brand strategy; and create brand awareness. Each is discussed below.

The Brand Launch Decision

The first step in the process of branding a health care system involves a conscious decision to launch the system as a brand, not to be confused with launching a product. Again, products come and go, brands endure, and at the core of any health care product the customer or prospect should be able to distinguish the brand's (i.e., the health care system's) system of values and meaning. Further, it must be recognized that brand launch is not synonymous with product launch, and as Kapferer writes, "the new brand must be thought of as a full identity prism from the start–in other words, we should focus on the functional and nonfunctional values which it incorporates."[6]

Create Brand Identity

It is reasonable to say that in the health care industry, and in particular among health care systems, few organizations have a brand identity or even know the difference between brand identity and organizational image. Image is a function of how customers or prospects decode the various tangible elements of market excitation (i.e., advertising, community involvement programs, public relations, etc.). Identity is a function of the health care system, where the meaning, intention, innovation, and individuality of the organization are consciously developed and manipulated to produce competitive advantage.

Brand identity is not merely visual identity, where colors or logo design or print styles are the basis for brand communication. In the health care industry, the issue of brand is not one of graphic appeal, rather, it is one of "speaking" to customers and prospects in a manner by which the intrinsic values and position of the organization are communicated and reinforced through all of the organization's activities–from creating contractual relationships between providers and payers to demonstrating affinity with the goals, motivations, and values of prospects and customers in nonverbal or visual ways.

This is not to say, however, that the outward appearance of the brand is unimportant or inconsequential; rather, the issue of brand identity must be addressed before formulating a visual identity. In fact, brand identity must be communicated using visual cues and messages allowing customers and prospects to quickly and efficiently distinguish between health care systems, their products, and intrinsic product attributes. In the changing dynamic, as a prospect or customer considers the actual features of a health care plan, the core values of the health care system as reflected in brand identity will drive the purchase decision.

According to Kapferer, brand identity comes from six sources: products, power of the name, brand characters and symbols, trademarks and logos, geographical and historical roots, and advertising (content and form).[7] Together, these form a "prism of identity," as shown in Figure 5.3, which can be used to examine a brand in detail.

Using the prism plus other factors, it is possible to define a checklist for assessing whether a health care system does indeed have a brand identity:

1. Does the system have a physique; that is, a prominent characteristic separate and distinguishable from competitors?
2. Does an image of the organization spring readily to mind when the system is mentioned?
3. Does the system have a personality or has it acquired a character? If the system was a person, how would he be described?
4. Is there a particular culture or myth surrounding the system, particularly one which gives it a unique and marketable character?
5. When the customer selects the system, does he do so on the basis of how it reflects upon his self-image? Does selection of the system contribute to the composition of the customer's self-image?
6. Does the system offer an image of the type of customer that is a user of plan products?

7. Does the system appear to suggest a unique and special relationship with its customers, distinguishable from those of
competitors?
8. Does the system have individuality?

Using these characteristics within the prism of identity, Figure
5.4 shows a hypothetical example of a healthcare system, seeking to
differentiate itself around a family doctor/family medicine brand
identity.

Brand identity is the fundamental building block of *brand equity.*
Brand equity creates predisposition to purchase or selection, based
upon intrinsic values delivered by the health care system. In the
health care industry, these values may include such things as trust,

FIGURE 5.3. Prism of Brand Identity

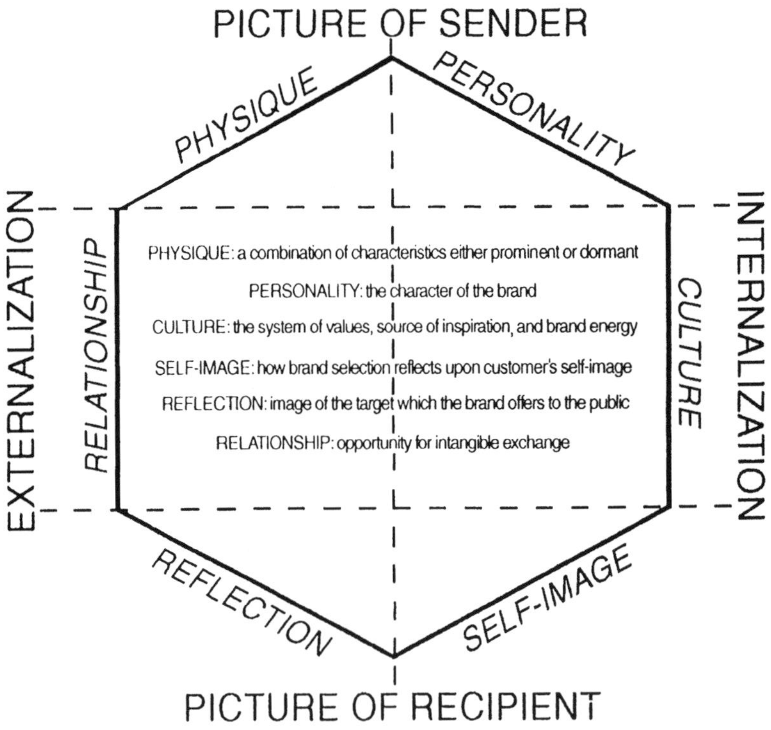

PICTURE OF SENDER

PHYSIQUE   PERSONALITY

EXTERNALIZATION   RELATIONSHIP

PHYSIQUE: a combination of characteristics either prominent or dormant

PERSONALITY: the character of the brand

CULTURE: the system of values, source of inspiration, and brand energy

SELF-IMAGE: how brand selection reflects upon customer's self-image

REFLECTION: image of the target which the brand offers to the public

RELATIONSHIP: opportunity for intangible exchange

CULTURE   INTERNALIZATION

REFLECTION   SELF-IMAGE

PICTURE OF RECIPIENT

FIGURE 5.4. Establishing a Brand Identity

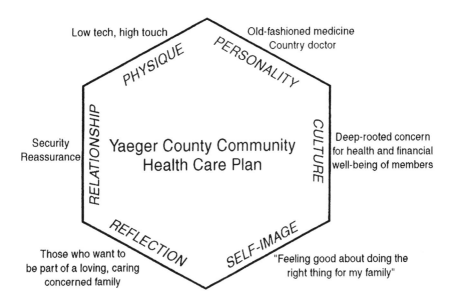

financial security, reputation for customer support, community responsibility, and so on. The brand equity "owned" by the health care system and the relationship of that equity to the goals, motivations, and values of the purchaser become part of the tradeoff exercise considered in the purchase decision.

Thus the health care system's brand identity is an intangible element, centered at the core of the organization's being. If the health care system's combined tangible benefits and brand identity is perceived by customers and prospects as consistently higher than any other system in the market, that system will have the highest customer loyalty in terms of purchase, repurchase, and recommendation. Competing health care systems can only improve their position against the market's brand equity leader by lowering their price in the short term, improving the tangible matures of products in the mid term, or improving their brand equity position in the long term.

Critical factors contributing to the definition of the health care system's brand identity should include:

- Understanding and rationale for the brand's existence;
- The system's unique and differentiated position in the market;
- The vision of the system as it relates to insurance, financial, and medical delivery aspects of health care;
- The core values of the system;
- The health care system's mission, particularly in regard to how it wants to impact customer's lives;
- Selection and marketing of products which best convey the system's mission and values;
- Selection of unique style and language and other image related concerns that will evoke favorable customer response.

Create a Brand Strategy

Brand strategy is a function of the relationship between brand and product, particularly in terms of what gets positioned (i.e., the brand or the product) and communicated and how that positioning is accomplished. If indeed brands serve to distinguish products and indicate origin, as the number of products brought to market by the health care system increases, the greater the need becomes for a systematic way to manage the relationship between brand and product such that they reaffirm one another and serve as mutually beneficial points of leverage in the minds of customers and prospects.

In the health care world, there are two basic models of brand strategy that might be considered by a health care system: a *Product Equals Brand Strategy*, where each product basically receives its own brand name and identity with little or no service paid to establishing brand identity or equity at the system level; or the *Shell Strategy*, where one brand identity is established at the system level that supports multiple products targeted to different types of customers and prospects.

Under a Product Equals Brand Strategy, as shown in Figure 5.5, an exclusive name and positioning is assigned to a product, and each product equals brand is managed differently from other products in the system's mix. It thus becomes the responsibility of the product manager to create a unique brand identity, create brand awareness and achieve brand equity for his product alone, regard-

FIGURE 5.5. Product Equals Brand Strategy

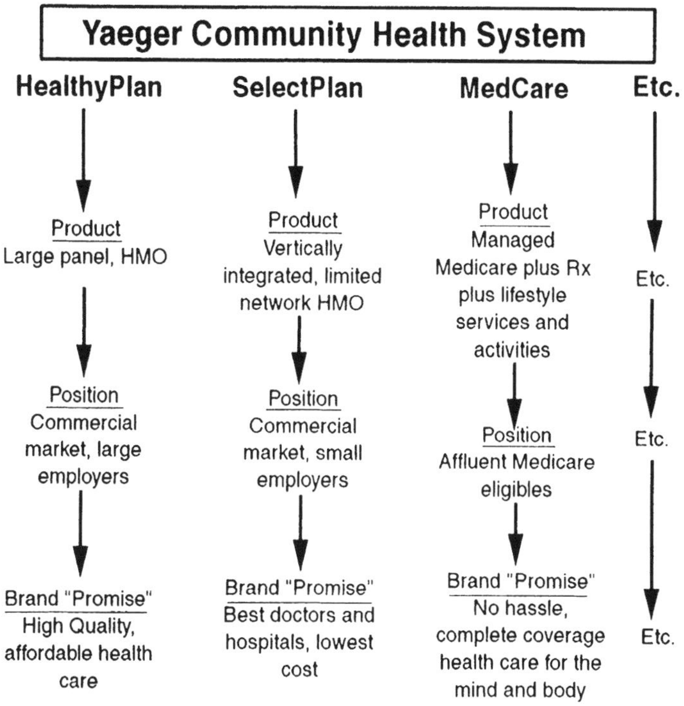

less of what other product managers are doing. The customers–be they employer or employee–purchase HealthyPlan, for example, on the basis of the product's identity, level of awareness achieved, and tangible features and benefits.

Under a Shell Strategy, as shown in Figure 5.6, brand identity and equity are accomplished at the health care system level, and products are brought together under one promise or position. In fact, the brand identity under this strategy serves as a launch platform for new products, where equity earned lowers market entry barriers. For example, Yaeger's brand promise of "old-fashioned health care delivered in a high tech way" works equally well as a promise for any type of commercial product, as well as for Medicare or Medicaid products. The notion of receiving "old-fashioned" health care creates a brand identity based around caring,

FIGURE 5.6. Shell Strategy

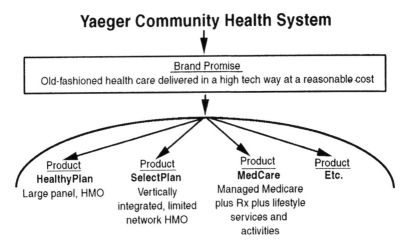

nurturing, concerned providers who put their patients' interests first, even if they have to hitch up the ol' horse and buggy and drive through a snowstorm in order to deliver a baby!

Of course, each type of brand strategy has different advantages and disadvantages, and will work best in different market situations. These are shown in Table 5.6.

Create Brand Awareness

The fourth step to the process of branding the health care system is to create and sustain brand awareness. Brand awareness relates to the number of persons recognizing the brand's significance, and who are conscious of the promise which this symbol expresses. As Kapferer writes, "A brand without awareness is but a blob on a product–voiceless and devoid of meaning. The aim of advertising is to reveal the meaning of the brand and to spread it as far and wide as possible in order to encourage people to try the products offered."[8]

Consider, for example, the Blue Cross/Blue Shield brand, a symbol promising tradition, stability, and health insurance that has been around for over fifty years. Blue Cross/Blue Shield has a very

TABLE 5.6. Comparison of Brand Strategy Options

Appropriateness	• Plans focusing attention on a specific target market • Plans that want to preempt a positioning and establish pioneer advantage	• Plans with limited marketing communications resources
Advantages	• Plan's brand portfolio is same as product portfolio • Each product gets precise positioning targeted to a specific segment of the market • One name per product helps customer see each one as different • Allows plan to take risks with new products, where failure will not impact overall brand identity • Provides greater flexibility to move into new markets	• Allows brand awareness to be shared by all products • Reduces cost of launching new products • Eases entry into new market segments • Creates strong image of consistency • Facilitates easier product line extension • Product managers get freedom to make detailed promises in line with their particular market segment
Disadvantages	• Only possible means of extension is to renew the product • Product launch = brand launch • Increase in number of product brands reduces opportunity for quick ROI	• Individuality of products may become blurred • Difficulty in finding single line of communications or position that will speak to all market segments • Overall brand will most likely compete against specialized and/or product/brands

high level of top of mind and unaided awareness in many markets, and of all the players in the health care industry, is perhaps best positioned to leverage this awareness into market dominance. Unfortunately, the Blue Cross/Blue Shield brand identity has not been particularly well managed over the years, and well-publicized problems have led to erosion of consumer confidence. Theoretically, Blue Cross/Blue Shield should be benefiting from "pioneer advantage"–the ability to capitalize and dominate a market based upon the fact that they were early market entrants with little competition.

Other companies, such as Met Life, New York Life, Travelers, Prudential, and a few others have attempted to extend their brand identity into the health care arena with varying degrees of success on a market-by-market basis. Here, their notion of leveraging their brand identity and the affinity they earned with consumers through other (nonhealth) products is, for the most part, strategically sound. However, virtually every national insurance company who has entered the health care market learned a hard lesson–that health care is a local market phenomena and that it takes more than brand awareness alone to motivate customers to purchase.

The opportunity to establish brand identity and create awareness is greatest in emerging and consolidating markets where the chaos of new relationships, alliances, and health system structures opens the door for pioneer advantage as customers have an immature system of preferences or a set of purchase criteria. The first health care system to create a branded identity and achieve high levels of top of mind and unaided awareness (both difficult and expensive as shown in Figure 5.7) will become the market prototype and a reference for all system brands that follow. This pioneer brand not only defines values and ideals for customers and prospects, but also, creates entry barriers for other brands from the perspective that they will have no other choice but to emulate the pioneer, thus facing a strategic handicap in terms of awareness. Brand awareness is a function of marketing communications (discussed in greater detail in the following chapter) and is closely related to the system's brand strategy.

BRAND EXTENSION
AND THE ART OF COMPETITIVE INNOVATION

Since competitive innovation is a way of thinking that cuts through the clutter of traditional health care marketing norms, once the health care system achieves a branded identity and awareness, thoughts might next be given to extending the brand beyond what might be considered traditional.

Since the brand has meaning, direction, and core values that

FIGURE 5.7. Levels of Awareness and Competitive Advantage

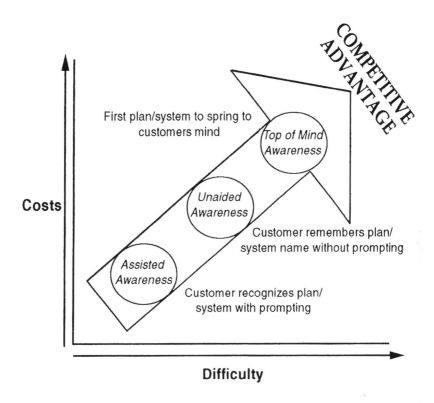

(hopefully) have created affinity with the goals, motivations, and values of customers and prospects, why not consider extending brand equity into other health care related categories? In particular, as markets mature and product opportunities decrease, the brand's equity can serve as a franchise of sorts, offering products and services that further cement the financial and health care needs bond between plan and customer.

Figure 5.8 shows an example of brand extension for Yaeger Community Health System, where the brand promise, "Old-fashioned health care delivered in a high tech way," has been extended to other product categories. Innovation, after all, does not necessarily need to rest only upon collection, analysis, and use of data!

FIGURE 5.8. Brand Extension

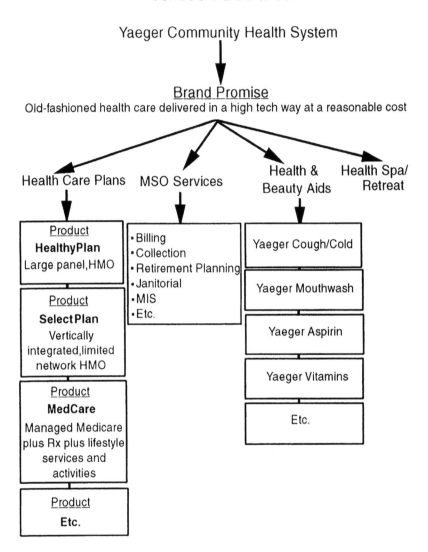

REFERENCE NOTES

1. *Competitive Strategy*, p. 4.

2. Michael Porter, "How Competitive Forces Shape Strategy" in *Strategy: Seeking and Securing Competitive Advantage,* eds. Cynthia A. Montgomery and Michael E. Porter (Boston: Harvard Business Review, 1991), pp. 11-27.

3. Eric Berkowitz, "Brand Equity Strategies" in *The Alliance Bulletin* (The Alliance for Healthcare Strategy and Marketing, March/April 1995), p. 3.

4. Jean-Noel Kapferer, *Strategic Brand Management* (New York: The Free Press, 1992), p. 2.

5. David Arnold, *The Handbook of Brand Management* (Reading, MA: Addison Wesley, 1992), p. 22.

6. Op cit., p. 74.

7. Op. cit., pp. 55-71.

8. Ibid., p. 88.

CHAPTER 6:
FIGHTING THE BATTLE—
THE ART AND PROCESS
OF MARKET EXCITATION

Don't think there are no crocodiles just because the water is calm.

—Malayan Proverb

The second component to achieving competitive advantage is paying attention to those external tactics or activities that represent the organization's front line on the battlefield. Labeled *Market Excitation* in Figure 6.1, because enthusiasm for product or service is key to securing competitive advantage, these factors must be built upon the strategic work and thinking accomplished in pursuit of competitive innovation.

There is an art and process associated with market excitation. The art of market excitation is related to the difficult decision making that must be accomplished relative to allocation of resources. Every single element of market excitation involves time, money, and people, all competing for a share of the organization's limited resources. Regardless of the type of IDN or health care system, these elements of market excitation are critical to success in the changing dynamic. Their absence or presence is not dependent upon type of health care market, rather, their execution may differ as a result of the strategic realities of the market.

Thus, resources necessary for developing and launching a new product compete for attention against resources needed for customer service. Or, the costs to expand distribution may compete against the costs needed to train and motivate a sales staff. Or, broadcast versus print advertising decisions may involve resolution of brand identity versus product marketing strategic needs. There is no particular formula or rule of thumb for allocating resources against these elements; hence, market excitation is an art.

The process of market excitation is more tactical in nature, involving a series of executional activities and programs designed for direct interface with customers and prospects. The key to under-

FIGURE 6.1. Elements of Market Excitation

MARKET EXCITATION

standing the process of market excitation is to understand that it is neither static nor formulaic, and will require continual experimentation and adjustment to reach the blend of resource allocation necessary to achieve the organization's marketing goals.

In order to secure competitive advantage and be a victor on the health care battlefield, all of the elements of market excitation—customer service, product mix, distribution, aggressive sales, and marketing communications—must occur. This chapter is devoted to exploring these issues.

CUSTOMER SERVICE AND SATISFACTION

The health care system's success in the changing dynamic will be dependent upon expanding the definition of "customer" and the effectiveness of customer service and retention programs and activities. One of the consequences of health care systems' concentration of marketing resources upon consumers is that "consumer as customer," may be too narrow a definition, and in the long run, this definition may adversely impact the plan's opportunity for success. Also, when marketing efforts are solely oriented to encouraging trial, programs and activities designed to encourage retention do not receive the attention and resources necessary to be effective.

In the changing dynamic, a *new* definition of customer must be employed: *a customer is any person, group, organization, or constituency that can impact choice, loyalty, or satisfaction.* Under this definition, a customer can be a consumer, an account, physicians, hospitals, community leaders, news media, and even the system's own staff. This expanded view of *customer* helps a system identify to whom to direct its marketing and marketing communications expenditures and suggests that a critical aspect of the system's success is not only to maintain and enhance current relationships, but to foster or create new relationships.

For example, several years ago we were engaged by an IPA HMO who discovered that physicians were influencing members to switch plans because of misperceived coverage limitations and occasional transactional problems. For example, one physician told patients to switch plans because her office staff was confused by coding procedures. Overall, our research indicated that if a provider suggested, or even outright requested the patient to switch, the likelihood of such a switch was over 80 percent.

To combat this effect, a "Strategic Provider Relations Plan" was developed with the express objective of enhancing relations with providers as a means of facilitating customer loyalty and for purposes of creating an environment for facilitating recruitment of additional panel members. Implementation of the plan involved four key steps: shifting toward becoming "provider friendly" in terms of actions, demeanor, and philosophy; enhancing communications efforts from quality and quantity perspectives; reducing administrative burdens; and reorganizing to improve communications and for purposes of eliminating inconsistencies in terms of fees and medical policy interpretations.

It thus becomes critical that each customer's needs must be identified in order to create the requirements for performance, and must be met in order to produce customer satisfaction and, ultimately, a quality product.[1] And, if a customer is defined as a person or organization or entity that has an existing relationship with a health care system, then retaining those customers, particularly in an environment of chaos, will be critical to the plan's success.

Roberta Clarke, Associate Professor and former Chairperson of the Department of Marketing at Boston University's School of Management, maintains that strategies to encourage retention receive little detail, yet:

> A well known American Management Association study, since replicated by many others, points to the conclusion that it costs five times as much to capture a new customer as to keep an existing one. Unfortunately, most health care organizations still define marketing as encouraging trial (capturing new patients or members) rather than retention. This is not a wise choice fiscally given the higher cost of attracting a new customer.[2]

Given this expanded notion of customer, it is apparent that the notion of customer satisfaction is both challenging and complex, requiring systems to define, measure, and demonstrate quality in new ways. Lois Bittle, for example, writes that:

The word *quality* relates to a subjective opinion where meaning is given to the word by the participant. In health care, the definition varies based on the individual or group providing the response. Each participant, provide, purchaser, and/or payer defines quality in operational terms based on its respective interests, priorities, objectives, and interpretation. The organization that defines this multidimensional concept of quality also determines the tools for measurement. For example, quality to a patient in the health care system is access and timeliness of service; to physicians, it is achieving desirable outcomes; to hospitals, it is financial viability and satisfied customers; to payers, it is the recognition that good quality equates to lower costs and customer satisfaction.[3]

Many health care systems have instituted Total Quality Management (TQM), Continuous Quality Improvement (CQI), or some other form of patient/member-based reengineering process management that is designed to deliver a seamless service and, if introduced to the organization correctly, to devote its efforts to building long term relationships with its customers rather than a series of one-time transactions.[4] Bittle writes that in a TQM/CQI environment, ". . . customers are viewed as anyone receiving a service throughout the organization. To continuously improve quality, each customer's needs must be identified in order to create the requirements for performance, and be met in order to produce customer satisfaction and, ultimately, a quality product."[5]

Allan J. Magrath, in *The 6 Imperatives of Marketing*, writes that "delivering products and services that consistently exceed customer expectations requires that (health care systems) first understand and measure these customer expectations. Only then can they monitor how satisfied these customers are with their performance and their competitors' performance on the same key dimensions."[6] Magrath postulates that customers evaluate suppliers in six general performance areas: overall product characteristics, price, quality of sales force, logistics, accessibility of support personnel, and overall reputation.

In virtually every one of these areas, marketing plays a big role. Consequently, achieving quality in marketing is a critical component of how a health care system can achieve and sustain competitive advantage. Figure 6.2, taken from *The 6 Imperatives of Marketing*, summarizes the central tenets of achieving quality in marketing. According to Magrath, "the outside circle highlights the importance of marketing leadership's commitment to quality, surveying customer expectations, and preparing quality plans and quality teams that can measure quality results. The inner circle underscores the importance of management processes such as front line marketing personnel empowerment, benchmarking, customer partnerships, and response time improvement."[7]

BROAD, EXPANSIVE PRODUCT MIX

The ability for a health care system to seize competitive advantage is also a function of an ability to deliver products and services

FIGURE 6.2. Processes and Priorities that Build Quality in Marketing

the market needs or wants. In the changing dynamic, this is a complex process that requires a balance of actuarial realities, competitive differentiation, managed care penetration, consumer comfort levels, and employer demands.

A tool for creating new products and product mix that has been used extensively in other industries (and sparingly in the health care industry) is *conjoint analysis*. Conjoint analysis is a technique for determining how potential buyers of a product or service value its various aspects or features which are referred to as attributes. The technique has proven equally useful for analyzing products and services in both the consumer and business-to-business markets.

Conjoint analysis assumes that a product or service is made up of various "attributes." Some attributes which might apply to health plan selection include:

- Physician offices
- Choice of doctors
- Health plan
- Office hours of physicians
- Premiums
- Services

Each of these attributes has several possible "levels." For example, the levels of the attribute "choice of doctors" might be: choose any physician, select from over 50 percent of community physicians, select from about 20 percent of community physicians. The levels of the attribute "waiting time at physician's office" might be: 15 minutes, 45 minutes, etc.

In conjoint analysis, potential customers are shown different versions of the product or service that are described in terms of specific levels of each attribute. Using various approaches, respondents are asked about their preference for various product/service concepts described in terms of these specific attributes and levels. By analyzing their levels of preference for product concepts shown, it is possible to estimate the relative value they place on each attribute/level. These estimated values are referred to as "utilities" or "part-worths."

These utility values can be used in choice simulators to make predictions about the choices that consumers will make among various versions of the product/service that are available or might be available to them in the marketplace. This analysis provides an opportunity to determine which particular product/service offerings will be most attractive to potential customers.

For selection of health plans, it is possible to identify the range of factors affecting decisions to join a system. Data can be manipulated to model cause and effect relationships. By defining new product prototypes in terms of the attributes and levels tested in the conjoint analysis, it becomes possible to assess the relative attractiveness of each prototype. Further, by correlating demographics or lifestyle data to the preferences, segments of buyers most likely to prefer a prototype can be identified, and the health care marketer can then tailor messages to those identifiable target audiences.

Generally, as shown in Figure 6.3, as markets move toward maturity, the number of products that a health care system must offer increases, but as cost and access considerations become moot, the number of products the system needs to offer decreases until such time that needs for plan and product differentiation drive creation of products around vertically integrated limited networks.

Many analysts agree that Point-of-Service (POS) products, combining managed care and indemnity elements (i.e., higher copays and deductibles for use of out of network physicians) are a necessary

FIGURE 6.3. Products vs. Market Maturity

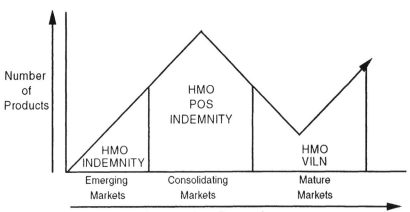

bridge for moving employers and consumers from indemnity to managed care coverage. The next transition, however, may be a movement away from managed care products with a broad, expansive medical delivery panel to one where selected physicians and hospitals are chosen to deliver a specific product–a *Vertically Integrated Limited Network* product where, perhaps, restrictive access translates to lower premium costs and higher provider risk assumption.

Key variables which need to be considered in the design of new products include:

- Benefits
- Premium
- Cost Sharing
- Participating Provider Panel
- Primary Care Manager
- Provider Reimbursement
- Ancillary Services
- Clinical Policies and Protocols

The interface of these variables represent a strategic (and actuarial) decision contributing to the design of a product. For instance, where payers desire greater control over quality and costs through a product that limits panel size and participation, the product needs to become more enticing to customers. Generally, this can be achieved through a combination of increasing levels of medical benefits, reducing or eliminating cost sharing, and reducing premium.

Developing a broad product mix is a function of the positive response of members (i.e., a limited product as one of a set of product offerings, flexibility, more options), employers (i.e., cost containment, more options for employees, total replacement), and providers (i.e., not locked out of the more flexible options, opportunity for financial reward if willing to assume to greater risk). In selected markets across the country, for example, a limited network product is even a *branded* product. That is, systems are using the concept of a limit and the characteristics of the limitation (i.e., who participates) as a means for marketing the product. However, it is important to note that these products are not "stand-alone"–rather, they represent one end of a continuum of products offered by the system as a means to increase market share.

Key considerations for designing new products include the following:

1. Respond to Market Pressures.

Consumers want choices and flexibility; they want to retain the right to make decisions about their health care after weighing their desire to self-refer versus the associated costs. Confusion can result when there are too many options; however, for the most part, consumers prefer a broad range of options ranging from tightly controlled/lower cost products to less controlled/higher cost products. Employers want to control their health benefit costs and want to have content and happy employees. Product options/variations such as POS, Specialty Select Panels, or Primary Care Managers provide cost control measures for employers while giving employees flexibility and choice.

2. Develop Participation Options for Providers.

Providers will respond favorably to participation in a system's product mix if given options for their participation; for example, greater financial risks equal greater potential for financial reward and more clinical control. Currently, payers seem to be proactive in establishing limited networks, generally "carved" from their entire panel. Essentially, they initiate the effort, extend invitations, and originate discussions about reimbursement and clinical guidelines.

However, as new forms of provider alliances are being created (i.e., PHOs, IPAs, POS, IDNs, etc.) as risk-bearing entities who are seeking contracts from systems, particularly in consolidating markets, it can be reasonably expected that these entities will proactively seek contracts and consequently (assuming that these entities will want to bear risk), the system may not need to "carve" a limited panel from its total panel–it may be done for them.

3. Consider Actuarial Risks.

Offering a stand-alone POS or other similar option against the competition may result in adverse selection as compared to offering a full range of options and the system must assess whether the potential for greater market penetration outweighs the risk of possible adverse selection.

4. Evaluate the Relationship of Product Pricing, Participating Provider Panel, and Benefits.

To attract members and to encourage the appropriate use of health care services, there needs to be an appropriate balance between the price of the product (premium and out-of-pocket costs), the provider panel, and the level of benefits. For instance, it has been suggested that the differential between the total cost to the member of in-plan versus out-of-plan services should not be greater than 20 percent in a POS product.

5. Create Premium Differentials by Adjusting the Size of the Participating Provider Panel, the Integration of the Providers, and the Type of Provider Reimbursement.

Premiums may be able to be reduced as control over provider reimbursement is increased and as the provider panel size is decreased. In addition, the development of a vertically integrated structure among participating providers (physicians, hospitals, ancillary) can have an impact on premium dependent upon the financial arrangements with the vertically structured entity.

6. Consider a Total Replacement Strategy.

While a limited network product may represent a marketable addition to a system's product mix, it also represents an opportunity—in conjunction with a POS product—to replace all products in an employer group and act as its sole carrier. Under this strategy, as the provider panel and flexibility to go outside the system increase, costs (premiums and out-of-pocket costs) should increase.

EXPANSION OF DISTRIBUTION CHANNELS

Simply stated, the key to enrollment growth for all types of health care systems is distribution; that is, being available and accessible to consumers, the ultimate end users. From the perspective of *commercial products*, this means establishing a presence at employers, using a direct sales force or through brokers.

The health care systems must, therefore, also develop and implement a marketing program dedicated to both employers and brokers—a key component of any overall marketing program which, sad to say, has received far less attention than marketing programs directed to consumers. Just like a consumer-oriented program, the system must have awareness, be positioned, differentiated, and speak to the goals, motivations, and values of the employer in order to be successful.

In order to expand distribution channels, health care systems need to consider what marketers in many other industries call trade or business-to-business marketing programs. These programs will require marketing communications expenditures for advertising, collateral, promotions, and so on. They will require special, value-added client and broker relations programs and activities. And they will need to be centered around a statistical communications platform, since employers are particularly concerned with a documented relationship between costs and outcomes.

Another possibility for expanding distribution channels is the opportunity presented by managed Medicaid and Medicare initiatives. Capitalizing upon these opportunities poses new challenges for the health care system from the perspective of both creating the medical delivery system and the fact that Medicaid and Medicare will place many systems in the unfamiliar territory of marketing directly to an end user with special needs and perspectives regarding health care.

In order to be successful in Medicaid and Medicare, the health care marketer must know the target market from size, geographic, and psychographic perspectives. Generally speaking, these targets will be significantly smaller in size than the commercial market, requiring less emphasis on mass media and more emphasis on grass root or neighborhood level marketing. A tool available that combines size, geography, and psychographics is PRIZMO© by Claritas Corporation.

PRISM© is a marketing tool that classifies every neighborhood in the United States into one of sixty-two distinct types or clusters, based around social rank, household, mobility, ethnicity, urbanization, and housing, allowing health care marketers to segment Medicaid and Medicare eligibles into groups to better understand their lifestyles and behaviors. By identifying neighborhoods where these types of prospects exist, and by having insights relative to purchase behaviors, marketers can develop target marketing plans focusing on these areas. At a local level, specific ZIP codes, census tracks, or block groups can be identified as areas of opportunity for site locations, outdoor advertising, special events, media buying, and direct mail activities.

AGGRESSIVE, MOTIVATED SALES STAFF

Even with expanded distribution channels, a broad product mix, customer retention programs, TQM/CQI processes, and the best strategic insights, a health care system's success requires the ability to seek out prospects and motivate them to a preferential purchase decision. The processes and outcomes of competitive innovation set the stage for sales (particularly in terms of defining product lines and mix, target markets, and market needs based upon market intelligence), but where the "rubber meets the road," so to speak, is the point and moment in time when the health care system's sales representative is sitting across the desk from a purchaser.

Sales functions and processes are becoming increasingly more complex as the dynamics of the health care industry change:

- Product lines and mix are increasing as is the complexity of products.
- Customers will have more choices of health care systems, abandoning current relationships for lower price or more benefits or better customer service.
- It is becoming increasingly more difficult to hire experienced sales staff, and sales training learning curves are becoming steeper.
- Difficult choices must be made between using brokers or an internal sales staff.
- Health care systems face the prospect of needing both business-to-business and retail selling staffs, as Medicaid and Medicare products are developed and launched.

The relationship of competitive advantage to sales processes and functions center around the execution of five activities (Organization, Management, Recruiting/Retention, Information Systems, and Training) and one key attitude–desire. Taken together, they comprise the STAR System of Sales as shown in Figure 6.4, and discussed below.

- *Organization* refers to the relationship between marketing (product and brand management) and the sales staff. The health care system may, for example, organize its sales functions around product lines (commercial, Medicare, and Medicaid) and make a determination of whether to use brokers or in-house staff.
- *Management* relates to both the system and processes of securing appointments, making presentations, closing sales, and recording sales information, as well as the function of managing sales resources to achieve desired outcomes or goals.
- *Training* is a critical aspect of the STAR System as the health care system's sales resources will need both product/technical knowledge and sales skills. The health care system must establish and maintain continuous sales training in order to be effective.
- *Recruiting/Retention* refers to a combination of tangible (i.e., salary, commission, benefits, etc.) and intangible (responsibility, autonomy, etc.) rewards that are necessary to both recruit qualified, experienced sales staff and to retain them. As competition in the changing dynamic heightens, so too will the competition for sales people who can bring the health care system's marketing goals' objectives to fruition.
- *A Sales Information System* is fast becoming a fundamental necessity for sale people in the health care industry, electronically providing on-the-job access to integrated information, advice, and learning modules as well as customer and document databases. According to Fetterman and Byrne[8] a number of improvements in efficiency and effectiveness can be realized by using an interactive selling system, including:

  -- improvements to close ratio
  -- shortening of the sales cycle

- ability to address more clients more effectively
- increase in customer satisfaction
- credibility for sales representatives
- reduction in sales support costs
- reduction in information distribution costs
- reduction in turnover costs
- increase in management's span of control
- reduction in training costs

The last element of the STAR Sales System is perhaps equal in weight and importance to all of the other elements combined–desire. After all, the true "bottom line" to competitive advantage is attitude, and at the sales level, attitude translates into a burning desire to win. William Murray, a Vice President of Corporate Learning Center maintains that "a salesperson's total performance is driven by two sets of factors. On the one hand, there are factors like product and technical training, and verbal and written communica-

FIGURE 6.4. STAR Sales System

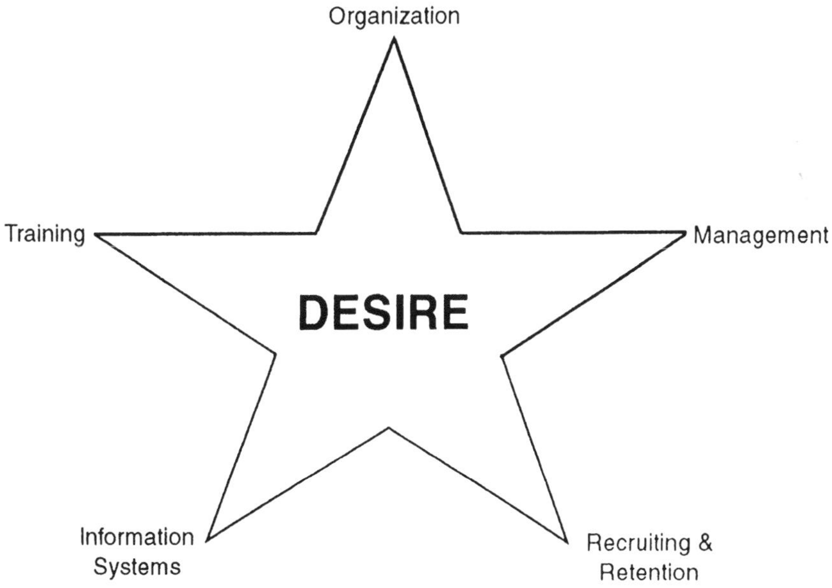

tions skills. These might be labeled a salesperson's 'potential.' The other half of the equation is the salesperson's attitude: potential is not truly effective unless it's driven by a winning attitude."[9]

MARKETING COMMUNICATIONS

Creating brand identity and awareness, and driving preference and choice through marketing communications are the more difficult responsibilities of the health care system marketer. Consider, for example, that a recent *Advertising Age* study found that on the average, people are exposed to some 5,000 commercial messages a day (from sources ranging from television advertising to logos on key chains), yet, when asked to recall brand or product names, less than one-tenth of one percent (about 50) came to mind.

Our lives are full of advertising clutter. We are continually bombarded with messages from countless types of advertisers via numerous types of media. Somehow, the marketing communications of the health care system needs to cut through this clutter, and deliver a memorable and motivational platform that will positively influence purchasers. No prospect is waiting with breathless anticipation for your television spot or brochure. The health care system marketer, through a combination of communications and creative strategies, must compete for share of voice and share of mind.

Tom McElligott, in an interview in *Inc.* (July 1986), maintained that somewhere between 95 percent and 98 percent of advertising just doesn't work because it doesn't break through or get by all of the other advertising clutter. When asked if there are any rules for developing the types of ads that break through, he replied:

> The rule, pretty much, is to break the rules. If you break the rules, you're going to stand a better chance of breaking through the clutter than if you don't. If you try to live with the rules, in all likelihood the work will be derivative, it won't be fresh, it won't have the necessary ingredients to disarm the consumer, who increasingly has got his defenses up against all sorts of advertising messages coming his way.[10]

Has the health care industry, in general, created advertising that is breakthrough ? After reviewing hours and hours of television and radio spots and reading countless numbers of print ads and collateral materials, my opinion is: NO. While I have seen communications materials with the highest of production values, the number of spots or ads or brochures that were truly compelling and motivating was quite limited. It is sad to think that the millions and millions of dollars spent on health care advertising may not have had the impact intended, and it is even sadder to think that as dynamics continue to change in the industry, the need for breakthrough communications will be even greater.

Issues related to creative executions are not the only marketing communications problems faced by the health care system marketer in the changing dynamic. Consider, for example, that:

- Choices must be made among different communications levels or strategies–economic (financial status of the system, annual reports, shareholder relations), institutional/image (corporate advertising, system philosophies, system culture), brand (identity, equity, and awareness aimed at purchasers not yet engaged in product comparisons), product (targeted straight to the consumer trying to make a purchase decision) , or category (managed care versus indemnity).[11]
- At least fifteen different audiences must be reached (employers, employees, Medicaid eligibles, Medicare eligibles, current members, staff, brokers, medical delivery system prospects, medical delivery system participants, shareholders, public opinion leaders, financial analysts, regulators, and so on) within a limited communications budget.
- In some cases, the communications process is continuous (Medicare and Medicaid sales; broker, internal, and member relations; and recruitment of medical delivery participants); in other cases the process is sporadic (annual reports, news releases, etc.), and in other cases, the communications process must be effected periodically around "open enrollment" schedules that may occur two or more times per year.
- The mix of products offered by any one health care system, particularly on the Second Generation Battlefield can be explosive, with each product requiring some level of communications support.

- Marketers are faced with a bewildering selection of media, including but not limited to sales promotion, point of purchase, print advertising, radio advertising, television advertising, outdoor advertising, collateral, direct mail, special events, and public relations.
- Media fragmentation has reached an all time peak; for example, the explosion of cable television, the plethora of specialty magazines, specialty radio stations, and so on has significantly complicated media selection decisions.

Amidst these issues, concerns, resource limitations, and other problems, the health care system still needs to develop and execute an effective communications program. In the changing dynamic, this will require a communications planning process including development of an appropriate communications platform or strategy, coordination and integration of marketing communications media, strategic and tactical decisions relative to media expenditures, and engaging creative executions. Each of these is discussed below.

Developing a Communications Platform

The communications platform is the central strategy or theme that ties brands to products while serving as a focal point for the health care system's message across all forms of media. It is the basis for creating integrated marketing communications (discussed below) and a tool for focusing creative energies for maximum impact upon customers and prospects. A communications platform captures the fundamental factors that influence or motivate brand and product selection, in particular, the goals, motivations, and values of a customer or prospect.

To create a communications platform, the health care system must:

- identify strategically significant, leverageable differences in the way customers and prospects think about the system and its products;
- develop a single-minded strategic focus which forges the most competitive, compelling, and motivating linkages between the system, its products, and its customers;

- show customers and prospects not only what products are, but how and why they are relevant to their business, personal, or professional needs;
- understand customers not simply as purchasers of a product, but in real, human terms;
- understand customer and prospect perceptions of and relationship with the health care system and its products vis á vis other competitive systems;
- go beyond simply telling customers or prospects about the health care system and its products to making the communications compelling and relevant to their needs.

The health care system's communications platform should be closely tied to the system's brand identity, and often, will be visibly reflected in corporate slogans. However, it is important to remember that even though a slogan can communicate the health care system's platform, it should not serve alone to carry the health care system's brand identity.

Integrated Marketing Communications

Because of limited budgets, changing market dynamics, multiple targets, and multiple strategic objectives, health care systems must be sensitive to maximizing the efficiency and cost-effectiveness of their marketing communications program. The concept of "getting the biggest bang for the marketing communications buck" is not a particularly new one, but in the world of health care marketing as in many other industries, traditional mass communications are increasingly less appropriate as audiences are increasingly more fragmented and disenfranchised.

In the packaged goods industry, for example, there has been a shift of dollars from mass media advertising to direct response advertising and consumer sales promotion.[12] Growing numbers of marketers are skeptical about the often ambiguous results of mass media advertising and traditional advertising communications models, and their emphasis on mediating consumer responses are giving way to behavior-oriented models that emphasize audience segmentation, customized persuasion, purchase incentives, and advertising accountability.[13] According to Nowak and Phelps, regardless of type of company or strategic orientation, we are witnessing a fundamental restructuring of the "rules" of marketing and advertising communication:

> The walls between the major marketing communications disciplines, namely sales promotion, direct response, and "brand" or image" advertising are collapsing, and marketers interest in *integrated marketing and advertising communications* is expanding. There is an increased marketer demand for multi-disciplinary campaigns, for advertising strategies that accomplish communications and behavioral objectives concurrently, and for creative executions that simultaneously generate awareness, promote market positions, encourage immediate behavioral response, and build customer databases that can be used to foster long term customer relationships.[14]

Just as *integrated marketing communications* (IMC) is growing in popularity in other industries, its application for health care in the changing dynamic is considerable. The American Association of Advertising Agencies (AAAA) defines IMC as:

> A concept of marketing communications planning that recognizes the added value of a comprehensive plan that evaluates the strategic roles of a variety of communications disciplines—for example, general advertising, direct response, sales promotion, and public relations—and combines these disciplines to provide clarity, consistency, and maximum communications impact.[15]

IMC proponents maintain that there are at least four interrelated changes in marketing communications strategy and tactics that accompany an integrated perspective: reduced faith in the power of mass media advertising; reliance on highly targeted rather than broadly targeted marketing communications; greater utilization of databases; and new expectations for marketing communications suppliers.[16] A principle tenet of IMC is that successful communications come from delivering the right message to the right customer or prospect, at the appropriate time, through the correct vehicle, at an appropriate weight.

Under the AAAA definition of IMC, the emphasis of communications is on producing "holistic" campaigns that draw upon brand/image advertising, consumer sales promotion, and direct response advertising in order to do whatever is necessary to identify, contact, activate, and cultivate individual consumers and increase market share. Marketing communications are therefore "integrated" to the extent they create a synergism that, at a campaign level, develops awareness, images, or beliefs while boosting behavioral responses beyond those that would be attained with a traditional one-discipline, one-message campaign.[17]

This type of definition and application works particularly well for health care systems who pursue a *Product Equals Brand* strategy. Using a Medicare product/brand as an example, an IMC approach might involve a combination of public relations, special events, direct mail, strategically placed outdoor advertising, and if appropriate, print advertising in neighborhood type newspapers. In this case, television or radio would only be cost effective if specific programs that can deliver a high reach against this target can be identified and bought. For a commercial product, the integrated approach would be different; for example, employers might be targeted with a combination of direct response (mail and print ads) and public relations in business publications, while employees might be targeted using broadcast and special events and so on.

Under a *Shell Strategy*, however, the concept and application of IMC must be revised. Here, integration would involve maintaining a clear and consistent image, position, and message across all marketing disciplines or tools, where the system's singular identity is reflected in communications strategy and executions that unify promotion, direct response, brand advertising, and public relations efforts. Unlike the product-equals-brand strategy, integration must be both horizontal (i.e., around the health care system as brand concept) and vertical (i.e., around products); but unified and coordinated in the sense that any communications, regardless of vehicle or target market or strategic objective, serve to reinforce and leverage brand identity, and create brand awareness and equity. Thus, public relations might be used to establish brand awareness, as part of a maintenance strategy for a particular product, or even to promote a product.

Perhaps one of the most intriguing aspects of IMC, yet least used by health care marketers, is the utilization of marketing databases. As health care system marketers increasingly segment and target customers, as demands for accountability and expenditure justification rise, and as the technological feasibility to gather, store, and analyze data can now be done cheaply using desktop resources, the use of marketing databases as a means to interact with customers and prospects has never been greater. In fact, in the changing dynamic, the use of marketing databases should grow exponentially.

Some examples of database marketing in the changing dynamic might include:

- Programs to up-sell or cross-sell existing customers, for example, targeting POS subscribers with a campaign to move them into a more tightly controlled managed care product using direct mail; or identifying current subscribers who, because of age, may be prospects for the system's Medicare products;
- Using geographic or psychographic based databases (like PRISM) to identify neighborhoods with high concentrations of Medicaid eligibles for purposes of delivering a targeted direct mail campaign or for placing outdoor advertising;
- Retention and loyalty building programs, to maintain or even increase the system's interactivity with customers or for purposes of maintaining awareness;
- Re-capturing lost customers or identifying or communicating with high potential customers, particularly on the commercial side relative to employers;
- Identifying and focusing upon high utilizers or members at risk because of lifestyle habits, and delivering medical programs or services that concurrently improve their health status and cement loyalty.

Communications Expenditures

How much to spend and what to spend it on are two of the more complex questions related to market excitation and securing competitive advantage. No health care system has an unlimited communications budget, and even large national companies who theoretically can achieve some economies of scale in marketing communications production, may not realize the same economies in media selection and buys as local market conditions will drive the strategic and tactical needs of the system's communications program.

There are six basic ways for the health care system to establish a marketing communications budget as shown in Table 6.1, each with specific applications, advantages, and disadvantages.

The decisions about what to spend the budget on should be a direct reflection of the internal and external analyses of competitive innovation. Assessment of market condition or situation (emerging, consolidating, mature) should reveal needs or opportunities for category growth, product/brand differentiation, or brand differentiation; or opportunities for competitive differentiation around product features or benefits; or even niche market opportunities where pioneer advantage can be obtained. In turn, this will define the most appropriate target markets and ultimately, media selection and schedule; but more important, will drive the level, intensity, and orientation of expenditures into one of three categories: maintenance, brand, or strategic sales. Table 6.2 provides an overview of expenditure strategies.

As shown in Figure 6.5, in the changing dynamic, allocation of the marketing and communications budget to different expenditure strategies can be directly related to managed care penetration. As managed care penetration increases, increasing levels of funds must be spent on brand identity. In markets of low penetration, more funds must be spent against sales strategy. But regardless of market maturity, a budget for customer retention must be maintained.

A maintenance expenditure strategy can be applied to trade or retail communications; to commercial, Medicaid, or Medicare products; and within any type of market. Essentially, this strategy calls for maintaining brand or product awareness at the lowest levels possible with the least amount or most inexpensive communications support possible. Expenditures for customer retention, unless the system has a severe disenrollment problem, might best be considered as a maintenance program. Theoretically, the type of products receiving maintenance level support are those whose awareness or market share will not unduly suffer from a lack of sustained or intensive communications expenditures. A maintenance budget can best be established using a percentage of sales budgeting method,

TABLE 6.1. Marketing Communications Budgeting Options

Budget Methods	Applications	Advantages	Disadvantages
Percent of sales—historic	• Works best for brands on products that have been on the market for some time • Works best where a predictable sales-growth pattern can be established	• Based on experience of previous years • Simplistic • Limits spending to a reasonable figure	• Locks system into last year's business • May disregard inflationary pressures • Mechanical rather than an analytical process
Percent of sales—anticipated	• Works best for brands or products that have been on the market for some time • Works best where a predictable sales-growth pattern can be established	• Keys budget to current sales trends, government or industry forecasts, or estimate of competition's sales	• Optimistic sales figures may inflate budget • If actual sales exceed estimate, budget may be too low
Percent of profits	• Works best for brands or products that have been on the market for some time • Not useful if new products are to be introduced	• Allows for flexible decision on amount to be invested in communications	• Arbitrary • May not be enough if based on previous year's profits • May be too much if based on estimated profits, sales decline, or unanticipated increase in costs

Objective and Task	• Works for brand or products that are either new or that have been on the market for some time	• Most analytic • Based around trying expenditures to objectives • Facilities prioritization of budget realities against objectives • Keys spending to specific pre-determined goals • Flexibility to switch expenditures from product to product as conditions warrant	• Research time, effort, and costs
All available funds	• Works best for new companies or products	• Let's you "pull out all the stops" • May help in developing a base for future profits	• Make a mistake, you're dead!
Competition	• Defensively managed companies	• Lets competitors lead the way	• Difficult to survive by blindly imitating others

TABLE 6.2. Overview of Expenditure Strategies

Expenditure Strategy	Spending Level Objectives	Suggested IMC Components	Budgeting Method
Maintenance	• Minimal levels necessary to maintain brand awareness • Maintain levels necessary to maintain product awareness • Customer retention	• Public relations • Outdoor • Direct mail (i.e. newsletters, advertising) • Point of purchase • Collateral	• Percent of sales
Brand	• Investment (long term) to create brand identity and awareness	• Print and broadcast advertising • Public relations	• Percent of profit
Strategic Sales	• Capitalize upon niche market opportunity • Capitalize upon short-term product advantage to drive sales • Capitalize upon pioneer advantage • New Product launch • Penetration of new market • Highlight unique product or service feature/benefit for purposes of driving sales	• Print and broadcast advertising • Sales promotion • Marketing, public relations • Direct response • Collateral	• Objective and task

FIGURE 6.5. Expenditure Strategies

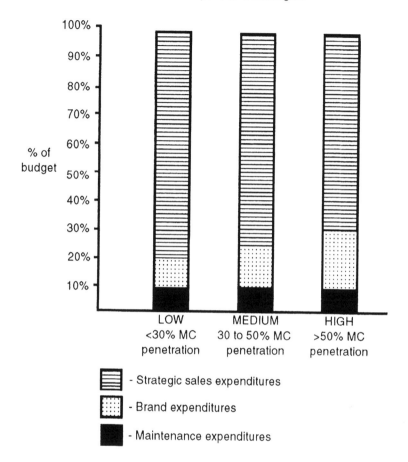

where spending levels can be based upon previous year's sales history.

Under a maintenance strategy, consideration needs to be given to reaching target markets in the most cost-effective manner possible. Here, targeted communications media such as direct mail can play an important role, particularly for customer retention purposes. Also, instead of using expensive broadcast advertising, a combination of public relations and outdoor advertising may suffice to maintain appropriate brand or product awareness levels. Even simple communications mechanisms such as point of purchase (i.e., posters at provider or employer locations) or collateral materials are cost-effective means of maintaining awareness.

The need for expenditures to establish brand identity and awareness were discussed in the previous chapter. Expenditures for brand identity are appropriate for any type of market and any target market, as long as positioning, identity, and communications platforms are consistent through all communications and within all product or campaign communications. However, as managed care penetration increases, health care system competitors consolidate, and product offerings are reduced, the need for brand expenditures will increase.

As mentioned earlier, establishing a brand identity and awareness is an expensive and long-term proposition. Here, mass communications media such as print and broadcast advertising are most appropriate, as the system's strategic goal will be reached, regardless of type of customer or target. Although expensive, when considered on a CPM (cost per thousand) basis, mass media is an effective way to invest system resources for brand identification purposes. In as much as brand expenditures are an investment, consideration might be given to using percent of profit as the basis for creating this type of expenditure budget.

Last, strategic sales expenditures must be a considered part of the budgeting mix. Here, the objective of all communications is single-minded—make a sale. As such, strategic sales communications are product oriented, intensive, timed to open enrollment processes where appropriate, or scheduled continuously as may be the case with Medicare or Medicaid products. Strategic sales expenditures might be used to capitalize upon a niche market opportunity, to highlight product features or benefits which are competitively advantageous, to leverage pioneer advantage, or even for purposes of penetrating a new market.

Of all the expenditure categories, strategic sales should receive the largest share of budget which can be spent in a variety of media including print and broadcast advertising, sales promotion (where appropriate and allowable), marketing public relations, direct response (particularly for a Medicare market and to a lesser degree, a Medicaid market), point of purchase, and collateral. Although receiving the largest share of budget, however, the percent of budget for strategic sales may be able to be reduced with market maturity as fewer products are strategically feasible or as product differentiation opportunities diminish.

Strategic sales expenditures will also require the greatest amount of strategic thinking and planning as market dynamics and market opportunities shift from year to year. Consequently, the objective and task method of budgeting is most appropriate for determining budget needs for this category of expenditure. The strategic and tactical requirements of splitting the commercial communications budget between consumer and business-to-business needs is a key responsibility of the health care marketer relative to strategic sales expenditures. According to Bob Beu, a Vice President at the Hutchins/Y&R advertising agency, "health care plans with low distribution need to focus resources toward employers, while in markets where a plan has saturated the employer distribution channel, significantly more resources need to be directed to consumer marketing" (Personal Communication).

As shown in Figure 6.6, splitting sales strategy expenditures relative to the commercial market is a function of distribution channel (i.e., employer) penetration: the lower the penetration, the more of the budget must be directed to trade programs.

Expenditure strategies and their relationship to integrated marketing communications will also differ dependent upon system branding strategies and objectives. For example, as shown in Figure 6.7, under a product equals brand strategy, expenditures by category of expenditure may differ from product to product dependent upon market situation, and each product may require different levels and types of communications support. Under a Shell Strategy, expenditures by category are set at the corporate level, and communications vehicles are selected, coordinated, and unified dependent upon the brand's overall strategic needs.

Engaging Creative Executions

The "rules" for creating good communications materials–user benefits in headlines, intriguing illustrations, clean typography, use of white space, and so on–are generally well known, and a review of health care marketing communications materials reveals that for

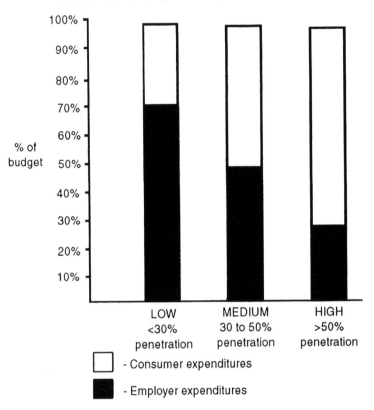

FIGURE 6.6. Splitting the Strategic Sales Budget

the most part, these rules are followed. But what separates that truly great ad from the run of the mill?

Fergus O'Daly, in *Sales and Marketing Management*, writes:

> Once in a while, you stumble across an ad that absolutely captures you. What is this elusive quality that can make one professionally done ad so much more effective than another? My word for it is "engagement." Some ads are simply more engaging than others. They engage you intellectually. Or emotionally. Or they engage your curiosity. However they do it, these all too rare ads instantly engage your full attention until you have absorbed the advertiser's message.[18]

FIGURE 6.7. The Relationship Between Expenditure Categories, Branding Strategies, and Integrated Marketing Communications

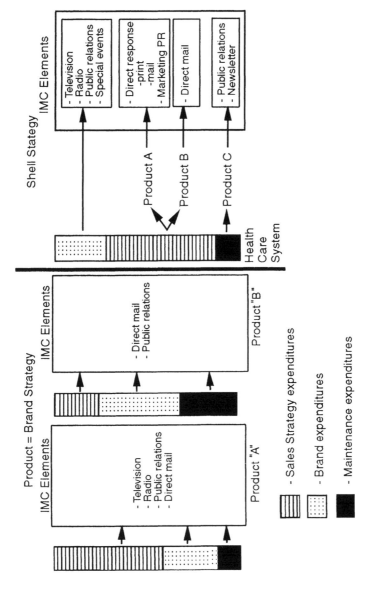

173

Achieving engagement is one of the most talked about and re-
searched topics in marketing communications. There's no formula
or routine, but according to Jim Morey of Young & Rubicam, it is
possible to define the qualities of exceptional marketing communications:

1. *Stopping Power.* "The premise, of course, is that if you can't
   stop them, you can't sell them. In this fast page turning, channel flipping world full of skimmers instead of readers, the
   prospect must be drawn into the ad within a second or two. He
   must literally stop, look and (ideally) become involved enough
   to want to know more."
2. *Simplicity.* "The greatest ads are the simplest. In great campaigns, there is an almost magical unity between words and
   graphics–a closure if you will–that seem both effortless and
   compelling. Companies think they want five different ideas
   featured in an ad; those multiple ideas become the enemies of
   simplicity. Simplicity is the mother of great advertising."
3. *Personality.* "Just as individuals have personalities, so do
   companies, brands and products. Just as we prefer the personalities of our friends to be consistent, we need to create and
   nurture personalities that reflect the enduring values of our
   brands and enhance ad recognition."
4. *Craft.* "You've stopped them in a relevant way. You've led
   them through a simple message that moves them. You've
   created a personality that fits the brand and builds recognition
   for its core values over time. Craft is the difference between
   mediocre advertising and advertising so involving that you
   relate to it viscerally even if you are not a prospect for the
   product. A brilliant concept poorly executed may succeed in
   some small way, but a brilliantly executed campaign can blow
   sales off the charts. Craft is what brings the idea to life, and as
   such is vital to the success of the campaign" (Personnal Communication).

Both the strategic and creative processes of marketing communications in health care should be guided by research and disci-
plined by marketing objectives, product offered, the media carrying

the communications, the target audience, regulatory guidelines, competition, and the opinions of anyone who must approve the communications. Perhaps the most important discipline is that the ultimate purpose of all marketing communications is to make a contribution to the adoption of whatever is being advertised.[19]

REFERENCE NOTES

1. Lois J. Bittle, "Quality Assurance to Quality Improvement: The Transition" in *Health Care Administration–Principles, Practices, Structure, and Delivery,* ed. Lawrence F. Wolper (Gaithersburg, MD: Aspen Publishers, Inc., 1995), pp. 429-446.

2. Roberta N. Clarke, "Marketing Health Care Services" in *Health Care Administration–Principles, Practices, Structure, and Delivery,* pp. 473-485.

3. Op. cit.

4. Ibid.

5. Ibid.

6. Allan J. Magrath, *The 6 Imperatives of Marketing* (New York: AMACOM), 1992.

7. Ibid., pp. 185-186.

8. Roger L. Fetterman and H. Richard Byrne, *Interactive Selling in the 90's* (New York: Ellipsys International Publications, Inc., 1995).

9. Arthur Bragg, "Why Salespeople Fail" in *Sales and Marketing Management,* Vol. 143, No. 8 (July 1991), p. 71.

10. "Adman Tom McElligott, Advertising's Hottest Creative Director Explains Why 95% of All Advertising Doesn't Work" in *Inc.,* July 1986, Vol. 8, p. 30.

11. A compelling argument might be made that category levels of communications can best be executed by trade organizations, for example, GHAA and AMCEA sponsoring national level ads to grow managed care, or a combination of the AMA, AHA, and HCIA sponsoring national level ads promoting indemnity coverage. This type of communications can also be effected on a coop basis; for example, markets with low managed care penetration can be targeted by the national association and production and/or media costs might then be split between the trade association and local health care system.

12. Glen J. Nowak, PhD and Joseph Phelps, PhD, "Conceptualizing the Integrated Marketing Communications' Phenomenon: An Examination of its Impact on Advertising Practices and its Implications for Advertising Research" in *Journal of Current Issues and Research in Advertising,* Vol. 16, No. 1 (Spring 1994), pp. 49-64.

13. Ibid., p. 49.

14. Ibid., p. 50.

15. Robert Tucker, "What is Integrated Marketing" in *Current Newsletter,* Vol. 18 (1995).

16. Ibid., p. 54.

17. Op. cit., p. 52.

18. Fergus O' Daly, "The Heart of Any Great Ad: Engagement" in *Sales and Marketing Management*, September 1989, Vol. 141, No. 11, p. 72.

19. Jack A. Bell, "Creativity, TV Commercial Popularity, and Advertising Expenditures" in *International Journal of Advertising*, Spring 1992, Vol. 11, No. 2, p. 165.

CHAPTER 7:
CONCLUSION

"(General Carl Von) Clausewitz viewed war as a rational instrument of national policy. The three key words 'rational', 'instrument', and 'national' are the key concepts of his paradigm. In this view, the decision to wage war 'ought' to be rational, in the sense that it ought to based on estimated costs and gains of the war. Next, war 'ought' to be instrumental, in the sense that it ought to be waged in order to achieve some goal, never for its own sake; and also in the sense that strategy and tactics ought to be directed toward just one end, namely toward victory. Finally, war 'ought' to be national in the sense that its objective should be to advance the interests of a national state and that the entire effort of the nation ought to be mobilized in the service of the military objective."

-Anatol Rapoport in an introduction
to Carl Von Clausewitz's work, *On War*

Although Von Clausewitz's theories of war are indeed too extreme to be applied *in toto* to the health care industry, one of his basic premises–that war is a rational instrument of national policy– has merit in the context of what has been discussed in *Marketing Health Care into the Twenty-First Century*.

Payer, hospitals, and physicians must initiate and execute strategies to secure competitive advantage based upon estimated costs and gains. And, in order to be successful, the entire organization must be mobilized and directed to this end. Consequently, now more than ever before, the health care marketer must assume an increasingly complex web of responsibilities on battlefields that are in a constant state of flux.

The entire history of health care marketing is fairly short. Until the 1970s formal marketing functions in health care were virtually nonexistent and professional health care marketing associations were not organized until the early 1980s. According to Dr. R. Scott MacStravic:

> Over its roughly two decades in life, health care marketing has seen itself questioned and criticized as undignified, inappropriate and ineffective. It has seen itself lauded as an essential and contributing force. Marketing staffs and budgets have waxed and waned repeatedly. Most recently, the demise of marketing has been announced as managed care and health care reform are supposed to make marketing functions unnecessary and superfluous.[1]

Pundits who have predicted the demise of the marketing function in health care are sorely mistaken. As the industry has evolved from the spendthrift days of the 1960s to the 1990s era of cost consciousness, so too has the marketing function. Today, and for the foreseeable future, health care marketing professionals face a complex challenge of fulfilling a "traditional" role (product development, pricing, packaging, promotion) within an environment of chaos, as new relationships are structured and as the battle for market share incorporates dimensions ranging from hostile regulatory environments to mega mergers and consolidations.

Traditionally, marketers in the health care industry have held responsibilities for product development and launch. From the payer's perspective, this translates into creating insured products around cost, benefit, and access variables. From the hospital's perspective, marketing has typically centered around promotion of services like birthing centers or single specialty services like occupational rehabilitation. From the physician's perspective, marketing has traditionally been ignored.

On the battlefields of the health care industry in the changing dynamic, customers are increasingly faced with a bewildering choice of options and coverages, copayments and co-insurances, in- and out-of-network benefits, and tradeoffs between cost and restrictions on access to physicians and hospitals. A product might be marketed and sold directly or indirectly. Its price may be based solely upon the experience of the customer, or upon the experience of the community. Consequently, the marketer is now faced with a multitude of different ways to package these products and a multitude of different types of customers, each with a different set of goals, motivations, and values relative to their purchase decision. And within any given local market, health care marketers may be experiencing a number of forces driving competition; for example, the threat of new entrants in terms of new payers and provider organizations, or the bargaining power of buyers, in particular, large employer groups.

Within this chaos, it will still be necessary for the payer, medical delivery, and health care system marketer to perform and concentrate on one primary objective: achieving competitive advantage resulting in motivating prospects (and customers) to preferential action. Given that any market can experience a number of different types of battles, each marketer's role will assume a heretofore unknown level of complexity, as each battlefield will be conditioned by a unique set of dynamics, strategic opportunities, and tactical marketing options.

Taking the position that in the changing dynamic everybody is a marketer, and given a focus upon the health care system as the product and/or brand, the roles and responsibilities of marketers must change, particularly as managed care pressures create new market dynamics and organizational structures. As markets evolve, the marketing function must be dedicated to strategic marketing analysis leading to creating relationships first, and based upon those relationships, creating products second. And, once relationships have been established, and excess capacity and utilization squeezed out of the market, influencing prospects to purchase may become a function of brand affinity and differentiation around access, composition of the medical delivery system, and brand identity.

The health care system marketer must therefore recognize and act upon the relationship between a market's evolutionary process and stage, and selection and execution of appropriate strategic marketing initiatives. Sun Tzu wrote in *The Art of War,* "The general who wins a battle makes many calculations in his temple before the battle is fought. The general who loses a battle makes but a few calculations beforehand. Thus do many calculations lead to victory, and few calculations to defeat; how much more no calculation at all. It is by attention to this point that I can forsee who is likely to win or lose."

In emerging markets, particularly from the perspective of the managed care organization, marketing activities on the battlefield should be directed toward growing the category; that is, moving people out of indemnity coverage to managed care. In consolidating markets, while category growth is still important, strategic marketing initiatives also need to be directed toward market share growth through product and/or brand differentiation, as the health care system competes for a growing pool of managed care prospects. In the mature market, where there are only a few large competitors who have the ability to quickly duplicate product innovations, market share growth becomes a function of brand differentiation.

Marketers in the changing dynamic must be willing to "break out of the box" of conventional thinking and norms. They must re-evaluate and rethink what health care plans are, what they do, and their fundamental meaning and value to customers. They must innovate the development of unconventional products or new ways of delivering and marketing existing products rather than expending energy simply to reproduce cost, benefit, administrative, or service advantages their competitors already enjoy. They must create and position differentiated, leverageable, and ultimately, marketable products through capitalizing upon market opportunities, the unique strengths or abilities of the organization as it currently exists, and competitive weaknesses. They must negate threats and create new capabilities driven by market need. They must be responsive to the evolving bargaining power of suppliers, as in the case of payers seeking to establish medical delivery panels.

The health care marketer of the future must hold an increasingly prominent, key position of responsibility on the battlefields of health care, for as Woodrow Wilson once wrote, "Responsibility is proportionate to opportunity." Marketers must, therefore, not only react to current market conditions, but also, be proactive in helping their organization understand and capitalize upon opportunities.

Robertson Davies once wrote that, "the world is full of people whose notion of a satisfactory future is, in fact, a return to the idealized past." Those who stand still, wishing for a return of "the good old days" face extinction. Those who face up to and take the dare of the future will have control over their destiny, surviving and even prospering on the battlefields of health care, leading their organizations boldly into the twenty-first century.

REFERENCE NOTE

1. R. Scott MacStravic, "The Health Care Marketing Function of the Future," in *Strategic Health Care Marketing,* Vol. 11, No. 6 (June 1994), pp. 5-7.

Index

Page numbers followed by the letter "t" designate tables; those followed by "f" designate figures.

Printed and bound by CPI Group (UK) Ltd, Croydon, CR0 4YY

23/10/2024

01777670-0003